Praise for

Healing IN THE KINGDOM

Cal Pierce's book is full of insights regarding healing and faith, healing and compassion, healing and transformation, and the possibility of walking in divine health. It is the story of what God can do with one man who is powerfully touched by God. When Cal stands before God, I am sure there will be a "Well done, good and faithful servant."

RANDY CLARK
Founder of Global Awakening

A divine encounter with God in 1996 made Cal Pierce set aside retirement and surrender to a mighty call of God. He is helping raise an end-time army challenged to do the works of Christ and even greater works. This anointed book will help activate you in doing these works of Christ in this strategic hour.

DR. MAHESH CHAVDA
Founder and president of Mahesh Chavda Ministries
Senior pastor of All Nations Church in Charlotte, North Carolina

As a forerunner, John the Baptist came teaching the message of the Kingdom, pointing to the one greater than he: Jesus the Messiah. Now my friend Cal Pierce also comes to us as a fore-runner, pointing believers in this generation in the right way: to the completed work of the cross of Jesus Christ, declaring loud and clear that healing is in the Kingdom! I applaud the ministry of the International Healing Rooms and thank the Lord for the deposit that this much needed book will make to the movement of signs and wonders in our day.

DR. JAMES W. GOLL
Encounters Network
Author of *The Seer, The Prophetic Intercessor, God Encounters, The Beginner's Guide to Hearing God,* and many more

We are in a changing season. Actually, we are changing from a "Church mentality" to a "Kingdom mentality." Cal Pierce, in his comprehensive, wonderful book *Healing in the Kingdom*, focuses us on how to see a Kingdom manifestation occur in our lives in the area of healing. This book will ignite your faith to be healed as well as to heal the sick. This is the healing manual for the generation and season ahead. Not only will you learn how your faith can heal the sick, but you will probably find out why you are having some physical issues. This is a must-read!

CHUCK D. PIERCE
President of Glory of Zion International Ministries, Inc.
Harvest Watchman for Global Harvest Ministries

What a powerful and refreshing word on healing for the local church. Scores of our churches do not have an intentional healing ministry. *Healing in the Kingdom* is a most practical and helpful guide to address the lack of healing prayer for the local church. I am so excited about using it in our seminars to raise up people who will do the healing ministry of Jesus.

TERRY TEYKL
President of Renewal Ministries

HEALING IN THE KINGDOM

Healing
IN THE
KINGDOM

How the Power of God and Your Faith Can Heal the Sick

CAL PIERCE

Regal

From Gospel Light
Ventura, California, U.S.A.

Published by Regal
From Gospel Light
Ventura, California, U.S.A.
www.regalbooks.com
Printed in the U.S.A.

Library of Congress Cataloging-in-Publication Data
Pierce, Cal.
 Healing in the kingdom of God / Cal Pierce.
  p. cm.
 ISBN 978-0-8307-4576-0 (trade paper)
 1. Spiritual healing. 2. Healing—Religious aspects—Christianity. I. Title.
 BT732.5.P54 2008
 234'.131—dc22

                                                                    2007039716

1 2 3 4 5 6 7 8 9 10 / 15 14 13 12 11 10 09 08

Rights for publishing this book outside the U.S.A. or in non-English languages are administered by Gospel Light Worldwide, an international not-for-profit ministry. For additional information, please visit www.glww.org, email info@glww.org, or write to Gospel Light Worldwide, 1957 Eastman Avenue, Ventura, CA 93003, U.S.A.

I dedicate this book to my son, David Pierce,
who went home to be with the Lord in February 1992.

Even though David battled muscular dystrophy,
he had a heart for Jesus. He was an inspiration to me.
Although in his wheelchair he could only move his
head and hands, he never complained, because he was content
in his relationship with Jesus. It was because of the intercession of
David for his mom and dad that we are where we are today.

David, we will never forget you.
It was your effectual prayers
that are now affecting the nations
(see James 5:16).

CONTENTS

FOREWORD

by Bill Johnson

In 1996, I was called to pastor the church that had sent us out in pastoral ministry 17 years earlier. The heart's cry of the church and its leaders was clearly for revival, no matter the cost. We were experiencing an outpouring of the Holy Spirit in Weaverville, California, where I had been for those 17 years. Within weeks of our coming back to Redding, a similar outpouring of the Spirit began.

After having a private meeting for my staff to introduce them to this move of God, I realized I needed to do the same for the leaders of the church that were not part of the staff. Around 100 people showed up to that gathering, where I gave a simple explanation of what had been taking place. Many loved it, others were confused and some rejected it altogether. I then invited the Holy Spirit to come—and He did. Many were touched in powerful ways. But the one person that would never be the same is the author of this book, Cal Pierce. Strangely, his encounter with God was one of the most important events of my life as well. I got to watch God take possession of a chosen vessel.

Cal and his wonderful wife, Michelle, had been a part of Bethel Church for 25 years. Yet they were planning on leaving. Somewhere around 1,000 others had made the same decision. While revivals are wonderful, they also cause problems, and they are messy. Not everyone wants to be in an environment where you don't always know or understand what is happening.

While Cal and Michelle came to the meeting that night because it was their responsibility as leaders, they were not supportive of what I was calling revival. But on that particular night, God had plans of His own. If ever I have seen the sovereign move of God over a man of His choosing, it was that night. He "fell" upon one who was not hungry for, interested in or even supportive of what God was doing. In so doing, He chose a vessel that would be forever faithful to His call and would impact the course of history for many nations around the world.

God took a bored board member and turned him into a primary spokesman for the healing revival that is sweeping the nations of the world. The restoration of the healing rooms ministry, while impressive, is but the tip of the iceberg. The Body of Christ is being equipped to do what Jesus did and teach what Jesus taught, in and out of the church setting. This is a great triumph!

Well over a decade has passed since that encounter. And Cal and Michelle burn even brighter with God's passion for the things that matter to Him. This book is the result of two surrendered lives pursuing the heart of God.

In *Healing in the Kingdom*, Cal has successfully captured the heart of the Lord for the restoration of healing to the Church as a normal part of everyday life. I love his no-nonsense approach to this subject. He confronts many of the objections that have been heralded through the ages and gives explanation to difficult passages, all adding credibility to this increasingly important ministry of the Church.

While many believers blame God for the lack of healing today, Cal puts the responsibility squarely on the shoulders of the people of God, where it belongs. The role we play in this important ministry is often devalued, as most would rather blame God than take responsibility. It's an important and bold step to wake up the Church to our role in affecting cities and nations in Jesus' name.

I also appreciate that alongside Cal's great focus on healing, he deals with the often forgotten truth called "divine health." We must have more on this subject. Cal's emphasis is needed and timely.

This wonderful book will help accelerate the training and equipping that is happening all over the world, putting another viable tool into the hands of the people of God that we might become all that Jesus intended. *Healing in the Kingdom* is sure to light an unstoppable fire in your soul for all that matters to God.

Bill Johnson
Author of *When Heaven Invades Earth*
Senior Pastor of Bethel Church in Redding, California

Truth
THAT SETS US FREE

HEALING FOR TODAY

We live in an era that has made more technological and scientific advances than any other period in history. The strides made in medicine in the past two decades alone are enough to set one's mind spinning—from our ability to see within the human body to detect disease and viruses, to unlocking the formula for life found within our DNA, to mapping the entire human genome.

It seems that these breakthroughs would enhance mankind's quality of life. But the sad reality is that in this age of hallmark discoveries, our health-care system is dangerously overloaded with the emergence of new diseases—such as SARS and Hepatitis C—as well as the reemergence of old diseases—such as tuberculosis, mumps and various strains of strep. In the midst of all this, the pharmaceutical industry has become a multibillion-dollar cash machine whose sole purpose seems to be to create medicines to eradicate these and other diseases too numerous to mention.

Does Jesus Still Heal?

Before we can demonstrate God's healing power to the world, believers must be *certain* that God indeed wants us well.

So how are we, as believers, to combat this onslaught of sickness and walk in the healing that Jesus provided for us? How can we live in divine health and show others around us how to do the same thing when we ourselves are still sick? Can Christians really lay hands on the sick and see them recover? Does Jesus still heal? These are just a few of the important questions that will be answered in the pages of this book.

As director of Healing Rooms Ministries in Spokane, Washington, I've personally seen over a thousand people *a month* come through the Healing Rooms seeking a touch from God. While the range of needs has been wide and varied, one thing that has caught my attention is that the majority of the people who desire healing are Christians. The obvious question is, *Why?*

It's amazing to me that in Jesus' day, the religious leaders didn't question Jesus' ability to heal or even to perform miracles but rather His ability to forgive sin. Yet over the course of some 2,000 years, the question no longer focuses on Jesus' power to forgive sin. Instead, as religious traditions have gradually saturated the Church like leaven, many Christians now wonder if Jesus still heals—and if He does, if He will heal *them*.

In Mark 7:13, Jesus reprimanded the Pharisees, telling them that they had made the Word of God of no effect through the tradition they were handing down. The reality is that the only way to destroy the barriers of tradition and unbelief, and to restore the truth of God's healing power to the Body of Christ, is to examine the only basis for truth—God's Word. I believe we need a strong, solid foundation, which can only be built upon the ageless rock of God's Word concerning healing.

What Is the Whole Truth?

It's time for us to relearn the truth about this often-misunderstood issue. In John 8:32, Jesus told us that once we know the truth, it will set us free—this includes freedom from misunderstanding the topic. This means that if we are not currently free, if we are still in bondage to pain, disease and sickness, then maybe—just maybe—we aren't operating in the whole truth of the Word of God concerning healing.

What we need in this hour is an application of the Word's instructions. We need an apostolic foundation that allows us to deal with the difficult questions people wrestle with in relation to divine health. We need a foundational understanding of healing that allows believers to move beyond just mere knowledge to the development of unshakeable, immovable *faith*. Jesus said, "Upon this rock I will build My church; and the gates of Hades will not overpower it" (Matthew 16:18). It takes a foundation of truth to make that happen.

In Spokane alone, we've had 70,000 prayer sessions, praying for and with people who come to the Healing Rooms. There, 140 team members from over 60 churches around the city are doing powerful work—laying hands on the sick and seeing them healed. As we progress in this work, we've seen every kind of disease healed. And while we have experienced an increase in healings, we must constantly pursue more. We must gain a better understanding of the things of God, apply them to our lives and then *do them*.

In past healing movements, where thousands would seek out great ministries, such as those of Aimee Semple McPherson, John G. Lake, Kathryn Kuhlman and Oral Roberts (just to name a few), the Church tended to push the work of healing onto the healing evangelists, operating under the false assumption that it was *their* responsibility to do the healing, not the Church's. I believe these past ministries were a vital part of God's plan to demonstrate His healing virtue. But they were not to be the sole source of His healing power; they were to be a catalyst that would bring the Body of Christ to a place of maturity, to a point of understanding its crucial role in divine health here on Earth.

Our dependence for God's provision of healing is not to be placed upon another person's gifting. In Mark 16:17, Jesus said, "These signs will follow those who believe" (*NKJV*). The signs follow, not only the powerful evangelist, the pastor of thousands or the eloquent teacher, but *all* those who believe. The Great Commission is a life assignment for every person who has accepted Jesus. That is why it is vital that all believers rise into their divine position of authority and begin to allow the Holy Spirit to manifest God's healing, miracles and power in the Body of Christ and throughout the world.

THE DISSING OF THE BODY

I believe that one of the reasons that we have lacked knowledge in this area is that we've experienced something I call the "dissing" of the Church by the enemy's camp. "Dis" was one name for the ruler of the underworld or hell in ancient Roman belief, and is another name for our enemy. The goal of "dissing" is to belittle something or to undo it. To take what is good and preface it with "dis" establishes *dys*function. It cancels what God is doing.

We have to break this *dissing* of the Church, because so often the enemy brings sickness, disease, poverty and broken homes into our lives to take the place of the health, joy, peace and eternal life God wants us to enjoy. Instead of having the ability in God to do all things through Christ who is our strength (see Philippians 4:13), we have *dis*ability. In place of the ease of God, we have *dis*ease. Rather than a divine appointment, we have *dis*appointment. Instead of being the connected Church, we become the *dis*connected Church. We no longer walk in belief but in *dis*belief. Instead of having contentment in God, we have *dis*content in the Church. And on and on. *Dis*courage rather than courage. *Dis*favor, *dis*order, *dis*passion, *dis*unity, *dis*comfort. It's a *dis*grace to the Word of God!

The truth is, it doesn't matter how much we've been dissed. God wants to take our *dis*appointment and turn it into our *divine* appointment, through the power of His Word.

The primary reason we have been dissed by the enemy is because of the way we approach God's Word. When we look to humanity rather than to God, or when we focus on the problem rather than the Problem Solver, we become dysfunctional and disconnected from the things of God. In the Body of Christ, we have a tendency to measure what a person does—or, more accurately, what the enemy does through a person—and to allow that to affect us rather than being affected by the truth of God's Word.

What causes us to do this? What makes us turn our attention away from God and toward humanity instead? The root cause is a critical spirit that puts our focus on those around us, ultimately disconnecting us from God's power and presence. We become critical because we look at what *isn't* working rather than what *is* working. We also tend to measure our future by our past, which will stop a move of God in our present and future. We become self-centered rather than God-centered, we get disconnected from the truth, and our reality becomes distorted. A critical confession then lines up with what the enemy is saying and doing to divide us rather than what God is doing to unite us.

A word that will bring healing to the whole of humanity by our whole God is needed from heaven to the Church. His truth on healing will lead us to freedom from the bondage of physical ailments and to a restoration of our place of divine prominence as the Bride of Christ. Equally important, it will bring blessings to those around us.

As you read the pages ahead, it is my prayer that your mind will open to the loving desire God has for us, His children. Freely embrace all He has for you without question and without doubt. Trust Him fully, for He wants only the absolute best for you.

1

THE *Mind* OF CHRIST

FILTERING GOD'S WORD

You can choose to live in the blessing or to live under the curse. You can walk by what you see and what you experience from the enemy's camp or by what you see and believe coming from God's camp.

The decision you make is based on what I call a "polarization between two opposing positions." These two positions cause people to filter the Word of God through either a Greek mindset or a Hebrew one. The Greek mind is what our democratic society functions under, and it causes us to react to what we *experience* with our natural senses. The Hebrew mind causes us to walk by a truth that comes from the *unseen* realm.

Second Corinthians 5:7 says, "For we walk by faith, not by sight." Jesus admonished us that the only way to live is "on every word that proceeds out of the mouth of God" (Matthew 4:4). It is our mindset that determines how we filter God's Word. One filter will cause us to measure the Word under the curse and the fall of man. The other filter will cause us to measure the Word under grace and redemption.

The Two Mindsets of Christians

Listed below are the polarizing positions between the two mind-sets held by Christians:

Mind of the Fallen (Under the Curse)	Mind of Christ (Redeemed by Grace)
1. Believes what is *seen* in a body	Believes what the Word *says*
2. Looks at humanity's *condition*	Knows our *position* in Christ
3. *Hopes* a person is healed	*Knows* a person is healed
4. *Wants* the healing	Wants the *Healer*
5. Follows *religion*	Follows the *revelation*
6. *Feels* defeated	*Knows* the enemy is defeated
7. Possesses *own* life	Possesses *His* Life
8. Justifies the *enemy*	Justifies our *God*
9. Seeks God's *hand*	Seeks God's *face*
10. Fears the *enemy*	Fears our *God*
11. Is *independent*	Is *inter*dependent
12. Believes it's about *me*	Believes it's about *Him*
13. *Seeks* the promise	*Lives* the Promise
14. Has a *rapture* mentality	Lives a *harvest* theology
15. Focuses on the *past*	Focuses on the *future*
16. Is *only* God's servant	Is God's servant *and* His child
17. Believes God's favor is *works based*	Believes God's favor is *grace alone*

Filtering the Bible through the blood of Jesus helps us to understand that we're free from the curse, just as Galatians 3:13 tells us: "Christ redeemed us from the curse of the Law, having become a curse for us."

Our Rightful Place

Redemption puts us in the proper position, but when we filter the Word through the Fall, we tend to *justify our condition* rather than *accept our position*. We offer excuses for our lack, brokenness, sickness and disease, or we justify the way we are rather than strive for the way we should be. We allow our confession to line up with the enemy's plan of death and destruction rather than with God's plan of life more abundant. We explain why we are sick, saying such things as, "I'm sick for His glory"; "He made me sick to teach me something"; "It's not always His will to heal."

Our position should be what redemption has provided for us: a truth that sets us free in every way! A proper position will explain why we are *already* healed: "By the stripes of Jesus I am healed!" (see Isaiah 53:5, *NKJV*). It puts our healing in the past rather than in the future. It says that we no longer have to live under the curse from which we've been redeemed. This is why *how* we examine the Word of God is crucial. We must look at it through the eyes of God's grace, which is His ability in us to destroy sin and sickness.

Redemption is a complete work. Jesus didn't go to the cross to redeem us halfway. He went to the cross to redeem us completely—in spirit, soul and body. To experience this complete work, we must choose to rise up and accept that place. Otherwise, we wear a morose "grave clothes" demeanor throughout our life rather than being clothed with the attitude of the "wedding gown" that befits the Bride of Christ.

Healing involves more than just physical healing. Healing applies to our mental and emotional well-being, as well as every other aspect of our lives. We know this because Romans 10:13 says, "For 'whoever calls on the name of the LORD shall be saved'" (*NKJV*). The word "saved" is translated from the Greek word *sozo*, which means "to save, keep safe and sound, to rescue from danger or destruction." A further study of the word *sozo* reveals that it also means "to save one suffering from disease, to make well, heal, restore to health." These explanations suggest that the word means "to be made whole." It's this wholeness that God wants to bring us into so that our spirit person is born again, our body is healed and our mind is renewed by the Word of truth. Thus, healing is not merely a physical restitution but a complete restoration of the whole person.

This is described in Romans 12:

> Therefore I urge you, brethren, by the mercies of God, to present your bodies a living and holy sacrifice, acceptable to God, which is your spiritual service of worship. And do not be conformed to this world, but be transformed by the renewing of your mind, so that you may prove what the will of God is, that which is good and acceptable and perfect (vv. 1-2).

The Word of God is so powerful that it can bring manifestation *before* transformation. Deliverance doesn't come with manifestation; it comes before that, when we receive the truth of God's Word as *rhema*—as not mere words on a page but as revelation knowledge that the Holy Spirit speaks to our hearts as His word for the specific situation we find ourselves in. Once we receive that *rhema* word and accept it as our own, then that truth sets us free. And when we're free, then God can use us as His vessel to bring His words of freedom to those around us who are in need. It is after we have been transformed and delivered that the fullness of God's Word and works is manifested in our life.

Becoming Familiar with the Spiritual Realm

As God's instruments of healing, we are also "a temple of the Holy Spirit" (1 Corinthians 6:19) and, therefore, the dwelling place of the Spirit of God. What does "a temple of the Holy Spirit" mean? According to 2 Timothy 1:14, it means that as followers of Jesus Christ, the Holy Spirit (one of the three Persons of our triune God) dwells within us.

In order for the Church to have a demonstration of the power that includes the manifestation of healing, we need to have the revelation of the Holy Spirit's work in the Body of Christ. We need to become familiar with the supernatural realm of which we are a part.

However, due to the filters of misunderstanding through which we base our beliefs, we too often read the Word of God but then go out and live our lives in ways contrary to what that Word instructs. As the Body of Christ, we must rightly perceive God's Word. In order to do this, we must first recognize that the Bible is living, powerful and creative, because it comes from the Creator, who is a supernatural God (see Hebrews 4:12).

Apostle Paul aptly stated, "But now we have been released from the Law, having died to that by which we were bound, so that we serve in newness of the Spirit and not in oldness of the letter" (Romans 7:6). We must live by the Spirit (which includes reading God's Word as a supernatural book and moving in the supernatural realm) so that we can receive all that God has in store for us.

Our Teacher, the Holy Spirit, wants to lead us into the truth of the Word (see John 16:13-15). The Spirit of God within us desires to bring power into our lives so that we can demonstrate His power on Earth (see Acts 1:8; Luke 24:46-48). But we can't get something *from* someplace if we're not willing to *go* there first. That is, we can't experience supernatural power if we won't go into the supernatural realm. And the truth is, we're already there, raised with Christ and seated with Him in heavenly places (see Ephesians 1:3,20; 2:6). The same Holy Spirit who raised Jesus from the dead and set Him at the right hand of the Father now dwells in us with resurrection power, giving us the ability to tap into the same power in which Jesus operated when He walked the earth (see Ephesians 1:19-20).

The Relationship of the Natural and the Supernatural

The natural realm and the supernatural realm are intertwined. Those who would try to separate the natural from the supernatural are those who would approach the Word with a religious mindset and Greek mentality. This neutralizes the power of what the Holy Spirit wants to do in and through us via the fruit of His presence, which brings the working of miracles and the gift of healing.

A religious mindset would have us believe in a system that causes us to think the devil has the power to make us sick and that God does not necessarily want to make us well. The truth is, God wants us to know that we have authority over *all* the power of our enemy, just as Jesus told His disciples:

Behold, I have given you authority to tread upon serpents and scorpions, and over all the power of the enemy, and nothing shall injure you (Luke 10:19).

This authority is part of our inheritance as believers, because we have the Holy Spirit *dwelling in us!* That's the seat of God's authority in the believer (see Ephesians 3:16-17), and it brings His kingdom to Earth (just as it is in heaven) as we fulfill His will here.

The supernatural and the natural are interconnected: The natural is an expression of the supernatural. In fact, the supernatural is more real than the natural, because God spoke and *then* the natural came into being. Thus, the supernatural preceded the natural. The only difference between the two is in what we *see*. In other words, the natural is the supernatural *seen* as it is demonstrated in the earthly realm. Christians will experience frustrations if they try to move the natural realm without the supernatural. Only by the supernatural can we fulfill God's will and establish His order in the natural realm.

The Light of God
Another way to look at it is to remember that God is light. There is no darkness in Him. When His light comes into our life, darkness is dispelled. In other words, darkness cannot exist in the presence of light. When we turn the light on in a room, darkness doesn't come in; it leaves. This same concept holds true for us, the believers. When the light of God's Word enters our heart, darkness—including such things as ignorance, unbelief, doubt and lies brought on by Satan—is dispelled. All forms of darkness are forced to flee in the presence of light. When the truth of the Bible illuminates our lives, then we become lights in the world, lights that illuminate the dark recesses of disease,

sickness and bondage and bring the Holy Spirit's healing, peace and power to those in need (see Matthew 5:14).

When we move into the supernatural realm, then we can fulfill God's will and watch the supernatural power of the Holy Spirit working *through* us to transform the natural realm.

The armor of God is really the armor of light. We "are the light of the world," quickened by the light of God, so that our armor extinguishes all the fiery darts that try to penetrate it (Matthew 5:14; see also Ephesians 6:16). In other words, attacks from the darkness are extinguished when they come into the light, because light overcomes the darkness.

In us, we have the power of resurrection to extinguish everything thrown against us from the camp of the enemy. The armor of light is the light of God in the believer, causing every bit of sickness to be destroyed because it cannot exist in the light.

Our focus must not be on what we see in the natural realm but on what we hear the Spirit saying to us from the supernatural realm. That revelation will bring the power of God to light up our life and overcome the darkness. Then we won't have to fight our enemy; the Holy Spirit will defeat him through us, because He who is in us is greater than he who comes against us (see 1 John 4:4).

The Wisdom of God

To overcome the things that have come against us from the enemy's camp, we must establish *vision* based on God's will for us. Once we know His will and begin to walk in it, then vision is established and comes into reality. All vision is birthed from the spiritual realm into the visible, natural realm in which we live.

It's the *demonstration* of power that the Holy Spirit wants to bring us into. That's why the apostle Paul said, "My message and my preaching were not in persuasive words of wisdom, but in demonstration of the Spirit and of power, so that your faith would not rest on the wisdom of men, but on the power of God" (1 Corinthians 2:4-5). It's that demonstration of power that gives us the authority to overcome the effect of the enemy.

In Ephesians 3:3, Paul stated, "By revelation there was made known to me the mystery." What is the mystery Paul is referring to? The gospel of salvation. God's Word is His will, and it is no secret that His will is for us to live a complete and abundant life. Yet the spirit of the world wants to negate the truth Jesus gave us concerning healing and deliverance—which is why we must seek God's wisdom for His will and direction in our lives.

Ephesians 1:17 tells us that "the God of our Lord Jesus Christ, the Father of glory," gives us the "spirit of wisdom." Wisdom is the proper application of knowledge. So it's the revelation of the knowledge of Jesus—the knowledge of who God is and what His will is for us. The spirit of wisdom will cause us to properly apply that knowledge so that it can be demonstrated in and through us to set our life in order and bring healing for our spirit, soul and body.

God's Word is so powerful that it can set us free before we even have the manifestation of our freedom from these physical ravages. God's desire for the Church in this hour is that we receive His Word with such power and authority in us that it causes us to take hold of His truth with a grip that no longer allows the enemy to infiltrate our thoughts with an unbiblical acceptance that God cannot or will not heal sickness and disease. It's being *set free* from unscriptural thinking that lays the foundation for bringing about the manifestation of healing.

And where does this entire transformation process begin? In the *mind*.

The Futility of the Mind

First Corinthians 2:16 poses a rhetorical question: "Who has known the mind of the LORD that he may instruct Him?" (*NKJV*) and then states our position as people indwelled by the Holy Spirit: "We have the mind of Christ." The mind of Christ is the spirit of revelation. It shows us who we are in Him, that we have been raised with Him and are seated with Him in heavenly places. He is our Head. Therefore, we have His mind.

When we read God's will as contained in His Word, we know what His mind is, because His will comes from His mind. And when we think and act according to the mind of Christ and in accordance with His will, God can work *beyond* what we could even think to ask, because it comes out of His kingdom.

> Now to Him who is able to do far more abundantly beyond all that we ask or think, according to the power that works within us (Ephesians 3:20).

In other words, when we have God's mind, we have His will. And when we function by the Word of God, we function in the will of God.

Ephesians 4:17 tells us, "This I say, and affirm together with the Lord, that you walk no longer just as the Gentiles also walk, in the futility of their mind." That "futility of their mind" is the Greek mindset, which would have us live according to what we *experience* with the natural senses rather than live by what we *believe* in the supernatural realm. This futility would have us read one thing in God's Word but live and believe another. It would have us live in the past, where previous hurts and pains dictate our present actions and where fear causes a past trauma to be a present reality. God's mind, on the other hand, encourages us to live for a future, with that vision ever before us.

It is this Greek mindset, this futility of the mind, that causes us to question God amidst our prevailing circumstances. When we try to function with "unrenewed" minds, we succumb to the waves of doubt discussed by the apostle James:

> Ask in faith, with no doubting, for he who doubts is like a wave of the sea driven and tossed by the wind. For let not that man suppose that he will receive anything from the Lord; he is a double-minded man, unstable in all his ways (James 1:6-8, *NKJV*).

Double-mindedness makes us doubt that God's Word is strong enough to apply to the circumstances that we're going through. However, no amount of pain, weakness, sickness or trauma in our lives is justification for doubting that the Word of God is fulfilled in us through faith. If our circumstances cause us to doubt, then our foundation was never properly set in God's Word in the first place.

Faith does not operate within the confines of circumstances; it moves beyond circumstances. Faith must always rest on what God has done, in order to renew our mind through His Word.

One of the greatest victories Satan can ever achieve is to cause us to take what he does and ascribe it to God. This happens when we say things such as, "Well, the Lord has made me sick for His glory," or the more popular cop-out, "God must have made me sick to teach me something." Statements like these put the stamp of approval on the devil's work and prevent us from receiving God's provision—all because of double-mindedness. We must renew our mind with the truth that *Jesus came "to destroy the works of the devil"* (1 John 3:8, emphasis added).

Renewing Our Mind: God's Power Is in Us!

How do we make sure that we are being guided by God's will and Word and not by our circumstances and the enemy's lies? Jesus said, "These things I have spoken to you that in Me you may have peace. In the world you will have tribulation; but be of good cheer, I have overcome the world" (John 16:33, *NKJV*). The way to overcome the enemy is to have our mind renewed by the power of the Holy Spirit, knowing that it is God's plan to bless, to heal and to prosper us (see Ephesians 4:22-24). Jeremiah 29:11 puts it this way: "'I know the plans I have for you,' declares the Lord, 'plans to prosper you and not to harm you, plans to give you hope and a future'" (*NIV*).

So often we forget God's order of things. We say things such as, "Well, I sure hope God is ready to fulfill His will. I hope I'm in His will." The truth is, God has already granted to us His precious and magnificent promises! We don't have to go through a regimen of spiritual calisthenics or good works to receive them.

Second Peter 1:3 says, "His divine power *has granted* to us everything pertaining to life and godliness, through the true knowledge of Him who called us by His own glory and excellence" (emphasis added). This passage says that God's divine power *has already granted* us everything we need. It doesn't say His divine power *might* grant us *some* of the things we need at some distant point in the *future*. Everything we need—everything pertaining to life and godliness—has already been bestowed on us.

We have a fulfilled life granted to us through the true knowledge of Him, which comes from a renewed mind. He has already given us all that we need so that we might "become partakers of the divine nature, having escaped the corruption that is in the world" (2 Peter 1:4).

Retaking Dominion

From the beginning of time, God's plan has been for humanity to take dominion. Satan gained legal entry into this world when Adam relinquished his authority to Satan after eating from the tree of the knowledge of good and evil (see Genesis 3:6; 1 John 5:19). But Jesus, through His obedience to the cross, came to restore authority back to humankind. That's why He said:

These signs will accompany those who have believed: in My name they will cast out demons, they will speak with new tongues; they will pick up serpents, and if they drink any deadly poison, it shall not hurt them;

they will lay hands on the sick, and they will recover (Mark 16:17-18).

Notice that this passage says that these signs will follow those who believe. It doesn't say *God* will lay hands on the sick; it says *we* will do that—because we are His Body. We are the works of the Lord's hands and the fulfillment of His will. As believers, we have the authority to put the devil in his place and take our rightful position of dominion in the earth. But if we don't have a mind renewed to understand our authority, then we will not properly exercise it when we need it most.

Jesus said, "The thief comes only to steal and kill and destroy; I came that they might have life, and have it abundantly" (John 10:10). Satan's plan is not so much to keep us out of heaven as it is to render us ineffective in the advancing work of God's kingdom here and now. If we are ineffective, then we can cause little damage to his reign of terror, which is why he desires to keep us in bondage, stuck in an unrenewed mindset that is contrary to the Word.

It is vital that you and I remember that we are no longer part of Satan's domain of darkness, but have instead been transferred to the kingdom of Jesus (see Colossians 1:13). When our mind is renewed to this truth, then we realize that we have not just been *delivered* but actually *transferred* to a new Kingdom. This is why we no longer have to accept sickness, disease, pain and infirmity from the enemy. We have been redeemed from every curse brought on by the fall of man and have been granted all of the blessings that come with the new Kingdom.

When we allow our mind to be overrun with thoughts of defeat and discouragement, then we fall prey to the lie that we are still operating under the curse. But when we discipline our mind in God's Word, we begin to realize that we are redeemed from the curse in order to be commissioned to go into all the world and minister the gospel.

God wants His kingdom manifested in the earth *now* so that we will have the power and ability to reap the final harvest. Sure, we will have a future kingdom, but we need the kingdom of God to be demonstrated with power on the earth *in this hour*. Otherwise, the enemy's camp will demonstrate its power against us. Romans 8:6 says it plainly: "The mind set on the flesh is death, but the mind set on the Spirit is life and peace."

When we have our mind set on Jesus and on the will of the Father, we are given peace. We're not moved by what the enemy does; we're only moved by what God does. In other words, even though we have an enemy in the world, he no longer dictates how our life is going to be, because anything that doesn't line up with the Bible is unable to shake the foundation of God's Word in our life. Instead of living in fear of the enemy, we think according to the Spirit, who attests to God's will for us. *That* is what a renewed mind looks like.

Fulfilling the Kingdom Vision

Jesus said that when the Holy Spirit comes, "He will teach you all things, and bring to your remembrance all that I said to you" (John 14:26). Through the Holy Spirit, we are connected to the Head, who is Jesus. We're His Body, and we have His mind. When we have the mind of Christ, our mind is renewed to the Kingdom of heaven and is not conformed to the earth, because we are seated with Jesus far above all principalities and powers. Now we have a *heavenly perspective*; we can see God's will for the earth and our role in bringing it to pass.

That's also why God gave us an imagination. With our mind we see vision, and with vision we have the ability to look forward. Vision sees what is ahead. Faith then allows us to fulfill that vision, because faith is the "engine" of the vision, of what we hope for (see Hebrews 11:1). Faith gets things moving so that the vision becomes reality.

When I was a little boy and would tell my mom something, sometimes she would respond, "Oh, that's just your imagination." I didn't believe it was my imagination; I thought I was seeing the substance of what I was hoping for. Vision is seeing what God has coming for us in the future, regardless of what happened in the past. That's why the apostle Paul told us to forget those things that are behind us and reach forward to those things that are ahead (see Philippians 3:13).

Vision is God's will for our future. When our will is God's will, our vision can be fulfilled. We become the fulfillment of our future when we walk by faith. When our mind is renewed to the Word, that renewed mind produces faith. It is that faith that creates the substance of our future. Thus, we walk by faith into our Kingdom vision, and the unseen realm becomes the seen reality.

Moving by Faith

Many people cannot see their future because they're too busy looking at their past. An unrenewed mind brings into focus everything from our past—especially failures, sins and short-comings. The truth is, we don't need faith to overcome our past, because it's just that—*past*.

The devil is the "god" of messed-up pasts, but Jesus is the God of fixed-up futures. That's why vision is forward looking, allowing us to see the delivery of what God has promised us. The world teaches that since we can't see our miracle, then it must not exist. But God's Word teaches that even though we can't see it, it *is* there—we know it is, because we have a vision of it and we're moving by faith toward it so that it can come to be.

There is something that God has prepared for us, something that we can only see with vision in the realm of the Kingdom. As we move toward that goal, or prize, by faith we will bring it from the supernatural realm into this realm.

But as it is written:

"Eye has not seen, nor ear heard, nor have entered into the heart of man the things which God has prepared for those who love Him." But God has revealed them to us through His Spirit. For the Spirit searches all things, yes, the deep things of God (1 Corinthians 2:9-10, *NKJV*).

KNOWING WE HAVE THE POWER

Only when we know beyond a shadow of a doubt that something exists in the supernatural realm can we then establish it in the natural realm. God wants to tap into our "knower," because before we can receive our healing, we must *know* that we're healed.

This knowing puts a demand on what is unseen and brings it into the physical world. When you *know* something to be true, then faith locks onto that truth and it becomes viable and kinetic, able to establish God's will upon the earth.

What we know in the kingdom of God (as revealed by God's Word) takes on creative force through us. But this can only happen as we become *doers* of the Word, because power is released in the doing, not in the mere seeing. Thus, it is what we do with what we don't see that determines what we eventually will see.

What we know in the Kingdom is greater than what we know in the natural. This is because the natural realm is subject to the supernatural realm of God—who created it. That's why in order to change our circumstances, we must apply the eternal principles of God's Word. The answer to our prayer in faith becomes the evidence of the unseen world of the spirit.

Tradition: Thief of Power

One of the things that keeps us from activating faith for our promise is tradition. Tradition is the thief of power. It makes the Word of God of no effect (see Matthew 15:6).

Religious tradition, based on a particular religious formula for receiving something supernatural, tries to compartmentalize our miracle. That's what Jesus faced with the Sadducees and Pharisees, and that same spirit is in operation today, trying to keep us from knowing truth. Religion cannot process truth because it establishes form and not power. It doesn't know what to do with power, because power creates change, and religion resists change. Religious tradition aims to keep things status quo, as they always have been, not inviting change.

Revelation, on the other hand, operates by *hearing*, which leads to establishing faith in your knower, so that change can come. Victory lies in our knower—we just have to put it to use. We already have the power, but too many in the Church simply don't know this truth.

Meditation: God's Word of Power

How do we develop our knower? By meditating on the Word to the point where it becomes a part of our very being. We don't just mentally assent to it, agreeing with it in our mind while questioning it in our heart. We internalize it and believe it with *all* of our being—body, soul and spirit.

God stressed the importance of meditating upon His Word to His servant Joshua, when He said:

This book of the law shall not depart from your mouth, but you shall meditate on it day and night, so that you may be careful to do according to all that is written in it; for then you will make your way prosperous, and then you will have success (Joshua 1:8).

Jesus also emphasized the importance of remaining in His Word. In John 8:31-32, He said, "If you continue in My word, then you are truly disciples of Mine; and you will know the truth, and the truth will make you free." To "abide" means *to continue*. If we don't abide, or continue, in the Word, then we might believe that God has the power to heal us, but we'll think He's not willing to. But when we do continue to meditate on the Word, we fully understand the truths God has spoken.

We must realize that with the Holy Spirit in us, we *too* have the power to put healing into effect at once.

In walking in the revelation of healing, we need to know that "the fear of the LORD is the beginning of knowledge" (Proverbs 1:7). This fear is not the kind of fear that will keep us checking our doors at night to see if they're locked. It doesn't mean being afraid of God—He is a loving God. The word "fear" in this proverb refers to *a reverential pursuit of God*, knowing that He has good gifts for us as His children.

When we begin with the Source of wisdom and knowledge, we are able to increase in the power of the Word that is in us, because we are abiding in it (see Proverbs 24:5). It's through that knowledge that deliverance comes (see Proverbs 9:10). The purpose of sowing the Word in our heart is to produce the power to bring deliverance into our life. That is part of God's design for His Word—to bring deliverance to His people.

But it's not enough to just have knowledge of God's Word; we must have *understanding* of it. Proverbs 14:6 says, "knowledge is easy to one who has understanding." "To have understanding" means to have wisdom or to act wisely with what God has given us. This knowledge and wisdom will open our eyes to the reasons God wants us to experience healing and to walk in divine health: simply because He's a loving Father and we're His children!

Think about it: If we have children, we don't desire to see them sick. We don't want to see them go through pain just to prove a point. It's the same with God. Healing is a natural extension of our inheritance as His sons and daughters. When we know this, then it's easy to step into and receive the benefits of belonging to His family.

One of the Holy Spirit's jobs is to bring us knowledge of the truth so that we're not tossed to and fro by every new teaching that comes along. When believers are submitted to the Holy Spirit, here is what happens:

This is the confidence which we have before Him, that, if we ask anything according to His will, He hears us. And if we know that He hears us in whatever we ask, we know that we have the requests which we have asked from Him (1 John 5:14-15).

Remember, it's what we know that determines what we have. If it's God's will and if we ask according to that will, then we will receive the answer to our prayers. It's important to know that we're not going to get our need met somewhere off in the sweet by-and-by, far in the distant future. We *already have* what we've petitioned the Lord for!

MOVING IN THE SPIRITUAL FLOW OF GODLY WISDOM

When we possess a spirit of wisdom, we also get a corresponding increase of power, moving us to act on what we know. When we receive the word on healing, then it is activated inside of us for the fulfillment of that word so that we can then receive our healing or impart healing to someone else.

Here are a couple of powerful Scriptures to stand on pertaining to the power of wisdom and knowledge in the life of the believer:

For the LORD gives wisdom; from His mouth come knowledge and understanding (Proverbs 2:6).

How blessed is the man who finds wisdom and the man who gains understanding (Proverbs 3:13).

Understanding causes us to have wisdom established in our life, and wisdom is the *proper application of knowledge*. Knowledge brings the past up to the present; and wisdom takes the present and moves it into the future, where it changes our life.

To the natural person, wisdom comes through time and the accumulation of experience; but to the spirit person, wisdom comes through the revelation of Jesus as given by the Holy Spirit. As the Holy Spirit comes and releases understanding of God's Word, it will set us free.

Here is how godly wisdom flows in each believer:

Wisdom comes when what the Spirit is saying is *heard* and *applied*.

↓

When wisdom is found, *understanding* is gained.

↓

Wisdom applies that knowledge to *drive the believer through every force of darkness* that is attempting to keep the believer from his or her miracle.

↓

Understanding then releases *knowledge*.

The great revelation here is that we're not limited by our age. We are only limited by how much we pursue the Holy Spirit. When we walk in the wisdom of God, we have the revelation that we are delivered, even before we receive the manifestation of that delivery—it's ours for the taking! Once we know this, then the words we speak will begin to change. Soon, each of us will confess, "I know Jesus bore my sickness on the cross, and therefore I am healed!" At that point, our confession then lines up with the knowledge of what God has already done to make us whole.

The Creative Force of God's Word

In order to move in God's power to see the sick healed, we must first *know* that we have the power to heal the sick. In other words, what we *know* determines where we go. Stated yet another way: The amount of our doing is determined by the amount of our knowing.

When we know the Word and we release it through ourselves, it ceases to be just the letter of the law or mere ink on paper, empty and void of power. Rather, it becomes a creating force spurred by our faith in God to accomplish what He sends it to do.

For example, we can prophesy God's Word of household salvation and watch our children (or spouse) accept Jesus as Lord and Savior because we know it's the will of God for them. We can speak to depression trying to cloud our mind and watch it disappear right before our eyes. We can tell sickness to leave our body, and experience total, instantaneous healing.

Perseverance is important, just as Jesus taught in Luke 18:1-8. Many people have been caught in a vicious cycle of releasing the Word, looking for a sign of instantaneous change, failing to see change immediately and then becoming discouraged and allowing doubt to enter—which is precisely what obstructs their answer! Even Jesus persevered in healing ministry, when He had to pray twice for the blind man in Mark 8:22-25 for complete healing of the man's blindness. And in Mark 11, Jesus said:

> Have faith in God. Truly I say to you, whoever says to this mountain, "Be taken up and cast into the sea," and does not doubt in his heart, but believes that what he says is going to happen, it will be granted him. Therefore I say to you, all things for which you pray and ask, believe that you have received them, and they will be granted you (vv. 22-24).

Doubt leaves God's Word *out*, whereas knowing sets it *in* to perform its work. If the Word of God is the will of God, then we must believe that it has the power in itself to fulfill itself.

The writer of Hebrews called Jesus "the radiance of [God's] glory and the exact representation of His nature" and adds that He "*upholds all things by the word of His power*" (Hebrews 1:3, emphasis added). Isn't that interesting? God upholds all things by His *Word!* When God's Word intersects the earthly realm, what it was sent to do—whether it is to bring healing, hope, joy or deliverance—is accomplished. That's why it is our job as believers to release God's Word, because we are His voice in the earth to bring about His will.

The Moving Force of God's Word
It's what we *do* that determines whether or not we will see a miracle. God's power in our lives comes through the anointing of the

Holy Spirit and is released when we step out in faith and *do* what the Word says. We can't just be pew sitters who never act on the Word.

Power, by its very nature, is a constant, moving force. It is not static or motionless. God's Word becomes creative and powerful through us by our *actions*, not by our simply letting it reside inactively inside us. When the power of the Holy Spirit flows out of us, it produces energy like dynamite; and when that dynamite comes into contact with our natural world, it explodes upon the scene to transform the lives of the hurting and the lost.

Jesus came to do the will of the Father—not to do away with the Old Covenant, but to fulfill it. When He was crucified, buried and rose again, He went back to heaven to sit at the right hand of God. That's why He said, "It is finished!" (John 19:30), because He had completed His Father's earthly mission for Him. He then sent the Holy Spirit to reside in all believers, and the Holy Spirit brought with Him a great transfer of power. Now *we* are to operate exactly as Jesus operated on Earth—and we will do even *greater things than He did* (see John 14:12)!

That power given to us from God through Jesus is amazing. We're not to be timid, powerless saints who let the devil run all over us. We're engaged in a war for our rights as children of God. We are to be mighty men and women of God who operate in God-given authority.

From the days of John the Baptist until now, the kingdom of heaven has been forcefully advancing, and forceful men lay hold of it (Matthew 11:12, *NIV*).

The Lord wants to take His Church to a new level of wisdom, understanding and power so that we can begin to release the word of healing—not only within the confines of the Body of Christ, but also into the sea of lost people who need a touch from Him. We are the vessels for God to impart this healing balm in the earth. We are the fulfillment of His Word to go into all the world (see Matthew 28:19 and Acts 1:8). That's why we have to lead the lost to Jesus. We have to lay hands on the sick. God is not going to come and do that—He *already* has done that. The responsibility for answered prayer now lies with us, stepping out in faith. On certain occasions Jesus said that the healing power of God flowed according to the active, persevering faith of those who He healed: "Then he touched their eyes and said, 'According to your faith will it be done to you'" (Matthew 9:29). God requires it of us; that's why He resides *in* us!

MOVING IN THE TRUTH THAT DELIVERS

In order to receive God's healing word, we have to know that healing is a *fact*. So often we forget this and buy into Satan's deceptions. We read one thing in the Bible pertaining to healing but then live out another, because we fall prey to Satan's lies.

In John 8:44, Jesus referred to Satan as "the father of lies":

He was a murderer from the beginning, not holding to the truth, for there is no truth in him. When he lies, he speaks his native language, for he is a liar and the father of lies (John 8:44, *NIV*).

Jesus, on the other hand, is *the* truth (see John 14:6).

First Corinthians 2:14 tells us that "the natural man does not receive the things of the Spirit of God, for they are foolishness to him; nor can he know them, because they are spiritually discerned" (*NKJV*). Natural people walk by sight, making a determination based on what they see. Natural people cannot understand the things of God, because they feel enmity toward the things of the Spirit. But for those who have been renewed, the Holy Spirit becomes our Guide and Teacher, helping us to rightly divide the word of truth and anointing us for the fulfillment of the Word.

> But when He, the Spirit of truth, comes, He will guide you into all the truth; for He will not speak on His own initiative, but whatever He hears, He will speak; and He will disclose to you what is to come (John 16:13).

The truth activated in believers brings into our lives the benefit of what Jesus provided for us. God's promises already exist in the spiritual realm, and by faith we apprehend them by calling those things that are not as though they are, thereby bringing them from the supernatural realm into the realm where we live (see Romans 4:17). Thus, faith, through the spoken Word of God released through our mouths, becomes the catalyst to bring the anointing of the Holy Spirit to bear upon our situation (see Mark 11:22-25; James 5:17-18; 1 Kings 18:1,42-45). This means that God's Word spoken through us is able to bring creative, miracle-working power to our bodies, minds and every other area for which we're believing.

When the world sees God's power demonstrated through us, they will then be drawn to Christ's presence, just as an entire city turned to God after Peter healed Aeneas (see Acts 9:34-35).

The Struggle Against the Enemy

What good is it to know that Jesus is our Healer if we don't ever experience healing? God gives us His truths and promises—including those that pertain to healing—so that we, by faith, might have them demonstrated in our lives. Everything in the Word of God is the will of God for His children, and if it's His will for His children, then His children should have it.

I believe the number one reason we so often don't have God's will in our life is that we don't *learn* and *apply* the truths God has given us to set us free—we're too busy believing the enemy's lies! That's the very reason the enemy lies to us—to keep us in bondage. Jesus made clear in John 8:31-32 that knowing the truth and applying it to our daily lives releases God's power to set us free: "If you hold to my teachings, you are really my disciples. Then you will know the truth and the truth will set you free" (John 8:31-32). The enemy comes to steal the Word by bringing what is opposite of the will of God. When we listen to the lies and begin to meditate on them, they then become a new basis for our reality. When we start to give voice to the enemy's lies, our lives are driven by seeds of doubt and unbelief instead of faith and victory.

The key is to remember that our struggle here on Earth is not primarily with flesh and blood but against spiritual forces:

For our struggle is not against flesh and blood, but against the rulers, against the powers, against the world forces of this darkness, against the spiritual forces of wickedness in the heavenly places (Ephesians 6:12).

When we try to fight Satan in the flesh, we'll always lose, because we're on his turf, where he's the expert. But if we attack him with "it is written," as Jesus did in the wilderness, then we'll win every time (see Matthew 4:1-11; Luke 4:1-13).

I recall one time when a man came up to me after a conference and asked, "Would you pray for me? The devil's been telling me I'm no good."

I responded, "My goodness, I'm not going to pray for you."

Incredulous, he asked, "Well, why not?"

"Because you're listening to the devil rather than to God," I told him. "Is the devil a liar?"

"Well, yes," the man said.

"Then why are you listening to the liar?" I asked. "There's no truth in him."

Here's a little secret Satan doesn't want us to know: If he tells us something, we must believe just the opposite and we'll be fine. So often people have a tendency to listen to the lies of the enemy rather than simply standing firm on God's scriptural truth—and then they wonder why they don't receive answers to their prayers. It's because they didn't *truly*, in their knower, believe that God would answer them in the first place.

Overpowering the Enemy

Jesus said, "You will know the truth, and the truth will make you free" (John 8:32). In addition to meaning *actuality* or *reality*, "truth" here suggests *dominion, might, power* or *strength*. Our job is to act on the Word of truth that God has revealed to us by His Spirit. But lack of physical evidence can cause the devil to try to plant in our mind such thoughts as, *I'm sick!*, thoughts that accept symptoms or feelings of sickness as unchangeable or unpreventable by God's power. To that, God gives us a truth that says something like, "No, you're not *sick*! Jesus bore your sickness, carried your pain, and by His stripes you are *healed*!" (see Isaiah 53:5; 1 Peter 2:24).

The lie is that we can't accomplish anything. The truth is that we can do all things through Christ who strengthens us (see Philippians 4:13). The lie is that we won't amount to anything, that we don't have a future or a destiny. The truth is that our destiny is already secure in Jesus.

We need to bring the truth of heaven's Kingdom into our lives. God is trying to get His will into His people, but because of our free will, we have to choose to believe God's Word in order for it to be realized in our life (see Mark 11:24). All truth has evidence—that's why it is called truth. The evidence of God's truth is released when we believe that we have received it by prayer and petition. In other words, by our free will we partner with God for His will to become evidenced in our life.

The Gospel of John records Jesus as saying, "Whoever lives by the truth comes into the light, so that it may be seen plainly that what he has done has been done through God" (John 3:21, *NIV*). He who practices the truth sees clearly. That's why James 1:22 says, "Prove yourselves doers of the word, and not merely hearers who delude themselves."

Avoiding Doubt

The promises of God form the entrance, the door, that allows us to partner with Him in His divine nature. The reality of this is found in Colossians 1:

> To whom God willed to make known what is the riches of the glory of this mystery among the Gentiles, which is Christ in you, the hope of glory (v. 27).

The degree to which we allow Christ to reign as Lord over our life corresponds to the amount of time we spend allowing His Word to take root in our spirit. If we neglect the Word, then there is no root in us to manifest or sustain our healing. After a while, bereft of any real proof, doubt will begin to settle in and our healing will be voided.

The fact that some people don't receive what God has for them does not mean that God's Word is untrue. It only indicates that there are barriers keeping these people from walking in the truth of God's Word. They may not believe the truth of His Word or may doubt that it applies to their situation, or they may have other spiritual blocks that prevent them from receiving, such as unforgiveness, bitterness or other unresolved issues. Confession of doubt is essential to receive our healing. Romans 14:23 says, "Everything that does not come from faith is sin," and James 5:16 says, "Confess your sins to each other and pray for each other so that you may be healed."

When we understand the power of truth, it becomes the foundation for us to receive our healing. Thus, doubt and other unresolved spiritual issues can void or block a healing.

SEEKING THE CREATIVE POWER OF VISION

God desires that His people walk in the fullness of vision, and the greatest vision we can have is when our eyes are on Jesus. No matter what vision God gives to a person, no one should ever turn his or her eyes from Jesus.

Proverbs 29:18 says, "Where there is no vision, the people perish" (*KJV*). The word "vision" means sight, dream or revelation. Vision enables us to see God's will and what He has in store for us. When vision becomes reality, then God's will is done. Once God gives us a vision of something that He has called us to do, then our faithful submission to His guidance and direction becomes the substance of that vision, bringing the vision to pass in our life.

Too often, people get discouraged because they connect the concept of *vision* with some kind of ministry or gift that they don't have. This leads them to think, *Well, I'm like a fish out of water. I'm in the church, and I don't have anything to do. I'm frustrated because nothing is happening.*

Our focus needs to change from what we *don't* have to what we *do* have. We all know the cliché "The grass is always greener on the other side." But the reality is that when we get to the other side, we realize that where we were wasn't so bad and that we just needed to see it from a different perspective. To get to a proper perspective, we need to keep our eyes on Jesus, listen to the Holy Spirit and be in a preparatory place. This is a lifelong process for every believer.

Lack of vision brings discouragement and hopelessness, causing us to believe that nothing in our life will ever change.

Every day is diluted into a life driven by circumstances and what's happening to us rather than a life of purpose, passion and power.

With the absence of vision, we cannot see ourselves doing anything significant. We go from one year to the next with nothing changing and with a lack of fulfillment in our lives, while those around us—in our families and in our communities—are crying out for a healing touch from Jesus. Vision is the establishment of God's will. Vision causes us to see ourselves healed so that we can say, "By the stripes of Jesus, I *am* healed."

Every believer needs a vision. Each one of us must seek God's direction daily for our lives. It's as easy as telling Him, "God, You reward those who seek You, so I commit to seeking You daily."

Putting Feet on Our Vision

Religious tradition wants us to believe that our destiny is the pew, when in reality our destiny is to minister to our coworkers, our neighbors, our family members and our friends. Our destiny is to go into all the world and spread the gospel of Jesus Christ. This takes God-given vision.

When we step out in faith to deliver the message of the Kingdom, our footing may seem unsure at times, but the Holy Spirit will guide us. It's just a matter of stepping into that process with the knowledge that He will direct our path and will reward us, because we have sought the increase of His kingdom first.

Kingdom vision requires *action*, because all success comes from vision that is acted upon. It doesn't do any good to see something in the spiritual realm if we don't do something with what we see. We must *act* on our vision.

But we must do more than simply *do*; we must first plan. Success requires a plan. Proverbs 21:5 says, "The plans of the diligent lead surely to plenty, but those of everyone who is hasty, surely to poverty." If we want success in achieving our God-given vision, we must plan first. Without a plan, poverty is the result. Poverty requires nothing of us—do nothing and we'll achieve it (see Proverbs 6:10-11; 24:33-34).

Uniting Through a Common Vision

Not only do we need individual visions, but we must also have a corporate vision. Vision unites the Body of Christ as we work together to fulfill God's will on Earth.

One of the greatest Scriptures for this hour is Matthew 6:10: "Your kingdom come. Your will be done, on earth as it is in heaven." These simple yet powerful words of Jesus should give every believer a vision of the Church's mission on Earth. This mission is to bring God's kingdom—through power and demonstration—to other people and to become witnesses of who God is to the lost and the sick.

Spiritual vision should always be 20/20. When our vision of God, His will and His Word is 20/20, we will see clearly. We will see what He is doing far away as well as up close.

When the Body of Christ operates in *division*, however, it means that our shared vision is divided. Our common vision fails when we become either nearsighted or farsighted. When we are nearsighted, we have a tendency to focus on ourselves, we can't see the needs of others, and we certainly can't see beyond the natural realm to the realm of the supernatural. We only see ourselves and what's right in front of us. And farsightedness is exactly the opposite. When we are farsighted, we're able to see the supernatural realm, but we fail to claim it and make it a reality in the natural realm. We neglect to appropriate those things that are ours.

This is why our spiritual vision must be 20/20.

If you've ever traveled, you know the importance of a map to help you get to your final destination. In the same way, clear spiritual vision is necessary to get us to where God would have us go. It's important to have vision in the Kingdom realm so that we can prepare today for the imminent fulfillment of that vision.

When our spiritual vision is clear, we know that what we do today will determine where we are tomorrow. But when we lose sight of our destination, then our vision is interrupted. Our way seems unclear. It's as if we're operating in darkness, which can lead to discouragement.

Spiritual vision always operates *beyond* the now. When we operate beyond today, we have no limits, because we're operating by faith in God's truth and we're living at the edge, out there with God, where he does His most exciting work. When we are moved by this Kingdom vision, we step into God's destiny for us.

Fulfilling Our Vision

Humans are creative beings. That's why we build things like cities, highways, homes, automobiles, jet aircraft. Everything we see around us was created in someone's mind and brought into reality by acting on that thought, that vision. Think about creation itself: God envisioned, spoke and created the entire earth and everything on it. In much the same way, when we function in the Word of God with vision, creation takes place in and through us.

> Beloved, I pray that in all respects you may prosper and
> be in good health, just as your soul prospers (3 John 2).

As the Scripture above indicates, anything that keeps us from having a healthy body or a prosperous soul is not God's will. Life, not death, is God's will for us. Blessing, not curses, is God's will. Righteousness, peace and joy in the Holy Spirit all belong to us.

Only when our will is God's will can our vision be fulfilled. The key is in keeping our eyes upon Jesus. When our eyes are on the Master, we will walk by vision, no matter where we start. If our will is submitted to God, then no matter what storms of life swirl around us, we will be propelled into the position of destiny that God has ordained for us.

We each have the ability to determine our own future, by linking our will with the will of God, knowing that the Holy Spirit will lead us into His truth. That truth will open doors and bring about divine appointments in our life, because He goes before us and is also our rear guard.

Only God's vision can overcome our past. Vision allows us to see the delivery of what God has promised us, birthed from the supernatural into the natural as we fix our hearts and our minds upon Jesus.

2

GOD'S WORD ON

Healing

HEALING IN THE ATONEMENT

Within the last century, the Body of Christ has slowly begun to take a closer look at the meaning of the substitutionary work of atonement Jesus provided on the cross, specifically in the area of healing and wholeness.

As we saw in the last chapter, God sent His Son to restore mankind to its original state of power and dominion, along with all the fullness and benefits that position offers. The work of salvation that the Father provided through His Son, Jesus, was to impact His children totally, not just partially. We have been redeemed from *all* the curse of the law, not just some of it.

As we learned, *sozo* (the Greek word for "saved," which appears 118 times in 103 verses of the Bible) implies *complete healing*, or *restoration to full health*. So when Jesus said that "God did not send His Son into the world to condemn the world, but that the world through Him might be saved" (John 3:17, *NKJV*), He was talking about bringing the world to complete wholeness—spirit, soul and body.

The word *sozo* is used when the story of the woman who had an issue of blood is told in the Gospel of Matthew:

> And a woman who had been suffering from a hemorrhage for twelve years, came up behind Him and touched the fringe of His cloak; for she was saying to herself, "If I only touch His garment, I will get well [*sozo*]." But Jesus turning and seeing her said, "Daughter, take courage; your faith has made you well [*sozo*]." At once the woman was made well [*sozo*] (Matthew 9:20-22).

This woman didn't come just seeking a healing. She came in search of restoration, to be made *sozo*, or whole. According to Jewish law, this woman was considered unclean and therefore forbidden from coming into contact with other people. Yet she pressed through the crowd to touch the hem of Jesus' garment. When she did, His healing virtue flowed from Him into her body. Along with physical healing, she also received wholeness—restoration of those things that she had lost—such as her self-worth and the ability to once again interact with family, friends and others in the community who she was previously not even allowed to touch. I believe that all of this is what Jesus was referring to when He said the words that have been variously translated:

- "Be of good comfort" (*KJV*).
- "Be of good cheer" (*NKJV*).
- "Take heart" (*NIV* and *NRSV*).
- "All is well" (*TLB*).
- "Take courage" (*NASB*).

The word *sozo* is also found in Mark 10:52, Jesus' answer to a blind man who came to Jesus seeking healing: "Jesus said to him, 'Go; your faith has made you well.' Immediately he regained his sight and began following Him on the road." And again the word appears in Luke 8:36, which describes the public's reaction to Jesus' moving a legion of demons out of the man from the Gerasene region and into a herd of pigs: "Those who had seen it reported to them how the man who was demon-possessed had been made well."

In each of these instances, the *sozo* healing that Christ provided was a complete healing. The blind man, having his sight restored, was now able to live life fully. The demon-possessed man from Gerasa, now freed from the demons that had plagued him for so long, could return to his family once more. The healings were complete—body, spirit and soul.

God does nothing halfway!

The *Sozo* Life

Paul told the Ephesians, "For by grace you have been saved through faith and that not of yourselves, it is the gift of God" (Ephesians 2:8). It is by faith that we take the *sozo* work that Christ provided on the cross and make it our own.

James 5:15 says, "The prayer offered in faith will restore the one who is sick, and the Lord will raise him up." Why does God want to raise us up? Because He's a Father who loves His children and wants to redeem them totally. That's why Jesus became the sacrificial Lamb and took upon Himself the sins of the world. His work on the cross was to restore to humankind what Adam and Eve had lost as a result of sin.

The great prophet Isaiah caught a prophetic glimpse of the atonement Jesus would bring when he spoke the following words:

> Who has believed our message? And to whom has the arm of the LORD been revealed? For He grew up before Him like a tender shoot, and like a root out of parched ground; He has no stately form or majesty that we should look upon Him, nor appearance that we should be attracted to Him. He was despised and forsaken of men, a man of sorrows and acquainted with grief; and like one from whom men hide their face, He was despised, and we did not esteem Him. Surely our griefs He Himself bore, and our sorrows He carried; yet we ourselves esteemed Him stricken, smitten of God, and afflicted. But He was pierced through for our transgressions, He was crushed for our iniquities; the chastening for our well-being fell upon Him, and by His scourging we are healed (Isaiah 53:1-5).

When we look at this passage carefully, we begin to truly understand the *sozo* life Jesus provided for us. Notice that verse 4 says, "Surely our griefs He Himself bore, and our sorrows He carried." Some religious leaders say that this only applies to the spirit of a person, but a study of the passage reveals that it applies to the physical body of a person as well. The Hebrew word for "griefs" in this passage is *choliy*, which means "calamity: disease, sickness" and comes from the word *chalah*, which means "to be weak, sick or afflicted." This is the same word used in

Deuteronomy 7:15: "And the LORD will take away from you all sickness" (*NKJV*).

Isaiah 53:4 adds, "And our sorrows He carried." The word "sorrows" is translated from the Hebrew word *mak'ob*, which means "pain," and includes mental anguish and emotional pain (see Ecclesiastes 1:18; Proverbs 14:13). It is the same word found in Job 33:19: "Man is also chastened with pain on his bed." *Mak'ob* is also used in Jeremiah 51:8: "Take balm for her pain" (*KJV*). Thus, a rereading of Isaiah 53:4 renders the verse: "Surely He has borne our sicknesses and carried our pain."

One can try to dispute the meaning of this Scripture, but the fact remains: Jesus bore our sicknesses, diseases and emotional pain so that we wouldn't have to!

Someone might say, "Well, that's the *Old* Testament. We have a New Covenant. We don't live under the Old Covenant anymore." But Matthew's Gospel says that what was spoken by Isaiah the prophet was fulfilled when Jesus "Himself took our infirmities and bore our sicknesses" (Matthew 8:17, *NKJV*). Jesus was sent to destroy *all* the works of the enemy (see 1 John 3:8), and He commissioned us to follow Him and to achieve that same goal—to overcome all that the enemy tries to bring against us.

It is vital that we possess this foundational truth. If we don't, then we'll be tempted to justify being sick rather than standing firm on God's promise of healing. Before we can really establish a prevailing faith for healing in the Body of Christ, we need revelation knowledge of God's Word to rid us of all the uncertainty concerning His will to heal.

What good is it for God to commission us to be born again, to go into all the world and preach the gospel, only to leave us sick and flat on our backs so that we can't do as He says? It's difficult to share the word of healing when we don't appropriate God's healing word for our own lives. That's why it's vital that we know for ourselves God's ability and His will to heal us and those with whom we come into contact on a daily basis.

Our Complete Healing

The Lord did not say He would heal some types of sickness but not others. From cancer to the common cold, every form of malady must bow its knee to the healing power of almighty God.

Psalm 103:3 tells us that He is a God "who pardons all your iniquities; who heals all your diseases." Note that it says *"all"* here, not "some." This is because the atoning work of the cross was complete when Jesus said, "It is finished!" (John 19:30). He wasn't indicating that it's just getting started. He wasn't trying to say, "Well, you get born again and then go take a beating from the devil for the rest of your life." No. The atonement of our Savior was finished for *every part of our being*—spirit, soul and body. No longer do we have to be bound by the shackles of just getting by, being up one day and being down the next and battling infirmity at every turn.

Christ is our Healer, and the work of healing is already done. The word of healing that He provided two millennia ago is as real and active today as it was then, because Jesus "is the same yesterday and today and forever" (Hebrews 13:8); nor will He void His Word to appease any denomination, tradition or unbelief that might try to deny its power.

In Isaiah 53:5, the prophet stated that the Messiah *"was* pierced through for our transgressions," that "He *was* crushed for our iniquities," that He *was* chastened "for our well-being" and that by His stripes "we *are* healed." It's done; it's past tense; we're there! Even Peter stated that Jesus "Himself bore our sins in His body on the cross, so that we might die to sin and live to righteousness; for by His wounds you *were* healed" (1 Peter 2:24, emphasis added). Peter wrote about healing in the *past tense*, meaning that Jesus already bore everything that would attack our body. Christ isn't *going* to heal us—He *already has!*

Our Enduring Confidence

People too often pray and believe for healing for a time but then lose confidence because they don't see something happening when they think it should. Yet the writer of Hebrews tells us what to do during times when our faith is being tried:

> Do not throw away your confidence, which has a great reward. For you have need of endurance, so that when you have done the will of God, you may receive what was promised (Hebrews 10:35-36).

In other words, we must not lose heart or become discouraged. God *will do* what He promised; He *will* bring great reward to us.

Many people lose confidence and miss their manifestation of healing because they turn their attention from Christ and His Word toward the symptoms in their body. Rest assured, Satan will bring symptoms to tempt us to sabotage our own healing, and we help him when we speak negative confessions, when our words describe our symptoms as if they are unchangeable, rather than speaking God's powerful Word over our bodies (see Hebrews 4:12).

We must not lose hope. Instead, we must hold fast to the Word of God and boldly declare it where our physical needs are concerned. Hebrews 4:12 says that "the word of God is living and active, sharper than any double-edged sword." We must use the word that is active and produces healing power, no matter what it looks like. In Matthew 16:21-23, it is clear that Satan planted the thoughts in Peter's mind to rebuke Jesus for predicting His own death in Jerusalem, because Jesus responded to Peter by rebuking Satan: "Get behind me, Satan! You are a stumbling block to me" (Matthew 16:23). When we, like Peter, allow our minds to accept and agree with thoughts planted by Satan—such as *I don't feel any better* or *The doctor said I'm getting worse*—then doubt is fighting against our faith, and our healing is in jeopardy of being voided or blocked.

Before we can receive our healing, we must believe it and then verbally declare it. Romans 10:10 says, "With the heart man believes, resulting in righteousness, and with the mouth he confesses, resulting in salvation." First comes the believing, and then the speaking. We can't speak first and then believe, because if the Word doesn't first take root in our heart, eventually we'll begin to doubt what we say with our mouth.

Think of the farmer who says, "Well, I believe God is able to give me a harvest," yet he's not willing to till the soil or plant the seed or water the ground! We have to plant the Word within us and give it time to germinate so that it can produce a harvest.

We live in a *now* society where we expect immediate results, but results don't always happen that way. They happen in God's timing, in accordance with His plan, and with our *action*.

The Soul's Healing

Sometimes God is not only interested in healing our physical body but also in bringing healing and restoration to our soul. That's why the manifestation of our miracle is, at times, gradual.

We often see this with people who visit the Healing Rooms. Many of them don't receive a manifestation of healing at the exact time they receive prayer. Why? Because God wants to do something in the *whole* person, not just heal them physically and send them on their way. He wants to build truth into them so that they will become spiritually strong bodies in the Lord and not weak and fleshly vessels susceptible again to sickness.

Remember the story of the paralytic man lying on a mat who was brought by his friends to a house in Capernaum where Jesus was teaching? The Gospel of Mark recounts the story:

> And they came, bringing to Him a paralytic, carried by four men. Being unable to get to Him because of the crowd, they removed the roof above Him; and when they had dug an opening, they let down the pallet on which the paralytic was lying. And Jesus seeing their faith said to the paralytic, "Son, your sins are forgiven."
>
> But some of the scribes were sitting there and reasoning in their hearts, "Why does this man speak that way? He is blaspheming; who can forgive sins but God alone?"
>
> Immediately Jesus, aware in His spirit that they were reasoning that way within themselves, said to them, "Why are you reasoning about these things in your hearts? Which is easier, to say to the paralytic, 'Your sins are forgiven'; or to say, 'Get up, and pick up your pallet

and walk'? But so that you may know that the Son of Man has authority on earth to forgive sins"—He said to the paralytic, "I say to you, get up, pick up your pallet and go home." And he got up and immediately picked up the pallet and went out in the sight of everyone, so that they were all amazed and were glorifying God, saying, "We have never seen anything like this" (Mark 2:3-12).

Notice that the house was so crowded that there was no way to get in to see Jesus. Well, where there's a will, there's a way: This man's friends took him up to the roof, removed the tiles and lowered him down—right in front of Jesus! They captured the Son of God's attention.

Riveted by what was happening, the crowd—and especially the religious leaders—listened closely. When Jesus said, "Your sins are forgiven," I can only imagine what the scribes and Pharisees were thinking! *Who does this young rabbi think He is that He can forgive sin?* Jesus' response was to say, in effect, "If you can't see redemption one way, then I'll show it to you in another. I will tell this man to take up his mat and walk." And the man picked up his mat and carried it off!

Everyone was amazed as they saw how salvation had impacted the physical man. And *that* is part of the *sozo* work of Christ's atonement: salvation for the entire person.

The Will of God

If sickness is actually God's will for some of His faithful children (as some believe), then wouldn't it be a sin to try to eject that sickness—to undo His will, so to speak? If sickness were God's plan, then wouldn't every doctor, nurse and hospital be defying Him by healing the sick? If some are sick because God wills it, then Jesus was defying His Father when He healed *all* that came to Him (see Matthew 4:23; Acts 10:38).

Redemption frees us from the law of sin and death. Romans 5:12 says, "Just as through one man sin entered into the world, and death through sin, and so death spread to all men, because all sinned." This proves that sickness is no more than a form of limited death; it's a death in progress, you could say. Sickness is part of the curse, and the goal of the enemy is to use sickness to take us out, to keep us under the curse. But since sickness is part of the curse, the only way that God could remove sickness was to remove the curse; and the only way He could do that was through substitution. That is why Galatians 3:13 says that Christ "redeemed us from the curse of the law by becoming a curse for us." Jesus had to become our substitute for the plague of sin, death and sickness so that we could choose Him and partake of everything pertaining to life and godliness.

Paul said it this way:

> For what the Law could not do, weak as it was through the flesh, God did: sending His own Son in the likeness of sinful flesh and as an offering for sin, He condemned sin in the flesh, in order that the requirement of the Law might be fulfilled in us, who do not walk according to the flesh but according to the Spirit (Romans 8:3-4).

If, as Romans 6:14 says, we "are not under law but under grace," and if grace is God's power in us to destroy sin and sickness, then why should anyone who is no longer under the law remain under the law's curse (of which sickness is a part)? That would be like keeping somebody in jail when they've been declared innocent in a court of law.

The truth is that the body is included in redemption. Isaiah 53:4-5 makes it clear that at the cross, Jesus made available to us the power not only to forgive our sins and redeem our souls, but also to heal and redeem our bodies: "Surely he took up our *infirmities* and carried our *sorrows*. . . . But he was pierced for our transgressions, he was crushed for our iniquities; the punishment that brought us peace was upon him, and *by his wounds we are healed*" (emphasis added; see also 1 Peter 2:24). Otherwise, there would be no resurrection. If we were resurrected with a body that is still under the curse, then we would be subject to sickness in heaven. But we are not; we are free from the curse and therefore free from sickness. Since our future destiny in heaven is both spiritual and bodily, then our redemption must also be spiritual *and* bodily— because there can be no bodily resurrection without bodily redemption. God is willing to show His mercy of healing to His own sons and daughters *now*, in this day and age.

The Father is glorified in what the Son has done (see John 14:13). When we receive the provision of healing provided by Jesus through the atonement of the cross, the Father is glorified because of what Jesus has done to bring that provision to us. The whole idea of the cross is that we benefit from it by receiving in faith what Christ did for us. And the only way we can access those benefits is by His grace (see Ephesians 2:8). No amount of good works can buy redemption or its benefits. That's why we must be renewed by the cleansing of our minds. We must rid ourselves of the idea that healing is only for others. It's for you and me, too!

The Answer to Prayer

A Healing Room is somewhat like a physician's office. The difference is that when people arrive in a Healing Room, they sign in and then receive prayer.

On one occasion, a lady who was in the latter stages of Lyme disease had heard testimonies about us from a friend, and she came with her husband and son for prayer. She walked with a cane and was experiencing much pain. At the house where she was staying, the bedrooms were upstairs and she had a difficult time climbing the stairs. She would have to take one step at a time and get both feet on a step before she could proceed to the next one. It even hurt to have her feet resting on the floorboard of the car as she traveled.

She said she came to the Healing Rooms in Spokane, thinking, *Wow—God's going to heal my body!* The team prayed for her, but she came out of the prayer room still experiencing the same amount of pain she had gone in with. The receptionist told her she could come back a second time, so she told her husband and son to wait while the team prayed for her once more. And again she left the room with the same pain in her body. She was visibly discouraged.

So often when we pray, we expect to receive the answer immediately. Many times we expect God to answer us on our terms, but that isn't the way He operates. He is sovereign, which means He alone is God—we are not. He will not be put into a box and told how things should work.

Thankfully, God had not yet written the end of this woman's story when she left Spokane. As she and her family started the drive back to her home in Idaho, her husband said, "Let's stop for dinner. I know how painful it is for you to prepare a meal." So they pulled into the parking lot of a restaurant, and they all got out of the car. As her husband and son started walking toward the restaurant, her husband noticed that she still stood by the car.

"What's the matter?" he asked her.

She responded, "Nothing—I can't feel any pain in my body!"

It seemed almost too good to be true. At dinner, she still tried to wrap her mind around the thought that she was actually healed. When they left the restaurant to drive home, she began thinking about climbing the stairs at their house. She thought to herself, *If I can just get up those stairs, I'll know I'm healed.*

The instant they pulled into the driveway, she was the first one out of the car. She went directly into the house and started going up the steps, one step at a time. With each step she began to go faster and faster, until finally she ran to the top and jumped up and down shouting, "I'm healed! I'm healed!" Then she ran back down and back up again!

The family came in and rejoiced with her. She and her husband walked a mile and a half that day, and three miles the next. The story was reported in the local newspaper with the headline: "Nationally known writer healed of Lyme disease in the Healing Rooms as the power of God began to work in her body."

This healing work of the cross is demonstrated in the lives of people as they rejoice in the Lord and give Him glory for what He has done in their body.

Another woman who came to a Healing Room had been bedridden for weeks because of acute back problems. Her pain was so severe that she had to have nursing care and couldn't even move. Her doctor said that the only solution was back surgery. But she had a friend who had heard about what God was doing at the Healing Rooms, and this friend called her up and said, "I want to take you to the Healing Rooms for prayer."

The woman responded, "But I can't travel. The pain is just too great. I can't even get up."

So her friend came up with a novel idea. She got a couple of men to place her on a mattress in the back of their pickup truck for the 30-mile trip to the Healing Rooms! Once there, the men literally carried her into the building, where they were met by a prayer team who immediately took her to a room for prayer.

The power of God came over this dear lady, and she jumped up off of the floor and came down instantly healed. Then she began to dance around the room. Now that's a God of healing! And the woman has been set free from every measure of pain in her back since then.

God desires that we get healed and stay healed, because He's a powerful God and He loves His children. We see this all the time in the Healing Rooms. It's an amazing thing to witness the power of God at work in the Body of Christ.

SAVING THE WHOLE PERSON

There have been seasons (or movements, if you will) in the Body of Christ that emphasized ministry to particular areas of need within the Church. First and foremost of these is, of course, the need for all to hear the message of salvation. This message has been heralded throughout the world since Jesus died and rose again. But sadly, the truth of healing, once prevalent in the Early Church, went through a downward metamorphosis from biblical fact to mere opinion, a bygone doctrine seemingly no longer relevant in the Body.

It wasn't until the mid-twentieth century that this vital truth of the gospel once again began to be proclaimed by healing evangelists across America. With God's healing power once again being preached and understood, the need to renew one's mind in the Word of God also returned to the forefront.

When Jesus comes for His Bride, He's not coming for a bride of failure. He's coming for a Bride in victory, a Bride without spot or wrinkle, a Bride that is sanctified entirely, having the spirit, soul and body made complete. This fact is supported by 1 Thessalonians 5:23:

> Now may the God of peace Himself sanctify you entirely; and may your spirit and soul and body be preserved complete, without blame at the coming of our Lord Jesus Christ.

Remember, we are the temple of the Holy Spirit, and God's temple should have no sickness in it. If Jesus bore our sickness on the cross, then why should we bear it? He bore it so that we wouldn't have to. I'm sure it grieves the heart of Jesus to know that His Body is still bearing the sickness He already vanquished.

Who wants us sick: God or the devil? Some might say, "Well, we have to be careful what we say so that we don't upset people who are sick." But it is a religious mindset that wants us to avoid speaking the truth in love and have an unbalanced sympathy for the sick. That kind of sympathy brings agreement and locks us in the sickness. Compassion, on the other hand, brings deliverance and takes out the sickness. Jesus wasn't sympathetic; He was moved by the compassion of deliverance to set the captives free and not keep them bound.

God loves us so much that He put His Spirit in us, and He is as interested in saving the physical person as He is the spirit of a person, but He can't use us if we get sick. If God were going to come and do the work He called us to do—to take the gospel of the Kingdom into all the world—then I guarantee that the work would have already been done by now. The only reason it hasn't been completed is because it's our responsibility to finish it, not God's. We're the ones who are to reach the lost, heal the sick and fulfill the will of God here on Earth.

DYING BEFORE YOUR TIME

It's not God's desire that our life be cut short. Psalm 90:10 declares, "As for the days of our life, they contain seventy years, or if due to strength, eighty years." This means that we're promised at least 70 years on this earth. Ecclesiastes 7:17 says, "Why should you die before your time?" God does not promise immortality on Earth, but He does say, "I will remove sickness from your midst" (Exodus 23:25).

God is a good God, and every good and perfect gift comes from Him. It's Satan who brings sickness and disease. It's Satan who wants us to be sick and to die before our time. He will even plant thoughts of death in our mind—thoughts of cancer, of heart attack or of other ailments. But we can combat him with such words as, "I will not die, but live, and tell of the works of the LORD" (Psalm 118:17).

Over and over throughout Jesus' earthly ministry, He taught about the love of our heavenly Father. Even the best earthly father will sometimes make mistakes with regard to his children. But our heavenly Father is perfect, never fails and always has our best interests at heart. He will withhold nothing from us, because He loves us so much. Jesus said it this way:

> If you then, being evil, know how to give good gifts to your children, how much more will your Father who is in heaven give what is good to those who ask Him! (Matthew 7:11).

The works of Satan are the "evil"—the sicknesses and diseases. God sent His Son "to destroy the works of the devil" (1 John 3:8). Too often we tend to justify what the enemy is doing to take us out rather than justify what God wants to do to keep us in the race. In other words, we become victims to our circumstances by justifying our sickness rather than repenting of any lack of faith, continuing to press in to God for our healing, and adjusting our actions to line up with the Bible (see Luke 18:1-8).

Remember, Satan wants to take out every believer he can, because he doesn't want us to expand God's kingdom. He knows that if our life is cut short, we can't fulfill that destiny.

KEEPING YOUR HEALING

The Bible teaches that we can lose our healing if we are not careful to walk in faith and repentance. In John 5:14, Jesus expressly warned the man whom He had healed of lameness that a condition worse than the first could come back on him if he persisted in sin: "Later Jesus found him at the temple and said to him, 'See, you are well again. Stop sinning or something worse may happen to you.'" Jesus' warning to the man suggests that just as a worse state of demonization may try to return to a person who has been delivered of demons (see Matthew 12:43-45; Luke 11:24-26), so, after one has been healed of illness, a worse condition than that which has been healed may be sent by Satan to try to regain lost ground and oppress us.

Each one of us must know how to receive our healing and keep it. In the Healing Rooms, we have people who come in, receive a healing and get excited and glorify God. But when they go home, the enemy tries to steal their healing by bringing a little ache here and a little pain there. If we have a problem with our foot, the enemy's not going to come and bring us a headache—he's going to bring the same pain in the same place that was healed, because he wants to cause us to doubt *that* healing. Satan knows that only seed that takes root in good soil can produce a bountiful harvest, so he wants to steal the Word *before* it can take root and produce a sustainable healing.

The one on whom seed was sown on the rocky places, this is the man who hears the word, and immediately receives it with joy; yet he has no firm root in himself, but is only temporary, and when affliction or persecution arises because of the word, immediately he falls away (Matthew 13:20-21).

When we receive healing as a result of God's Word, it must take *firm root* in us. Otherwise, the devil will try to re-afflict us with the very same symptoms to try to convince us that we are not healed and that God's Word is unreliable.

This attack of the adversary can be referred to as a *lying vanity*, which is nothing more than something that comes against us with the purpose of changing our mind. If the devil can cause us to look at the symptom instead of staying fixed upon God's promise, then he can convince us to believe his lie. When we focus on the symptoms and the pain, then doubt and unbelief come into our mind and give entrance to fear, which reestablishes the sickness.

To prevent this from happening, we *must* keep our heart and our mind fixed upon God and His promise and not on what the enemy wants us to believe. Isaiah 26:3 says, "You will keep him in perfect peace, whose mind is stayed on You, because he trusts in You" (*NKJV*). We are to hold fast to that which is good, allowing God's truth to take root in us so that it can complete the manifestation of healing in us.

The story of Jonah illustrates very well the meaning of a lying vanity:

Then Jonah prayed to the LORD his God from the stomach of the fish, and he said, "I called out of my distress to the LORD, and He answered me. I cried for help from the depth of Sheol; Thou didst hear my voice. Those who regard vain idols forsake their faithfulness, but I will sacrifice to You with the voice of thanksgiving. That which I have vowed I will pay. Salvation is from the LORD." Then the LORD commanded the fish, and it vomited Jonah up onto the dry land (Jonah 2:1-2,8-10).

Jonah chose to trust God rather than to believe a lying vanity, and it was then that God delivered him out of the belly of the fish. Had Jonah believed in the lie, he would have lost his faith and not received his deliverance.

If the symptoms of sickness return, then we are to reject the lie and set our faith on God and His Word—*no matter what!*

Symptoms of Sickness

What do we do when we have tried everything we know to try and we still have symptoms of sickness? If we don't have a solid position on what to do next, then we have a tendency to rationalize the way we are rather than verify what the Word can do.

Too many Christians know they're sick more than they know they're healed. On a number of occasions, Jesus said to people that healing would be released to them according to whether or not they believed it could be released (see Matthew 8:13; 9:22,29; Mark 10:52; Luke 7:50; 17:19; 18:42). This shows that healing can't even begin to manifest itself until doubt is completely removed and faith takes hold entirely.

The problem with many people is that what they physically see or feel too often determines how they respond to God's Word. But symptoms don't determine whether or not we're healed, only the Word does. Our symptoms of sickness should not tell us what we have; they should tell us what's coming: healing, through

God's Word. Our belief system will either focus on the symptoms of sickness or on the Word of God. The choice is ours.

The enemy has his own "gospel," which he preaches with symptoms and activates by fear. Unfortunately, too many Christians are busy buying into Satan's false bad-news gospel rather than the true healing gospel of Christ.

But the true gospel, activated by faith, is stronger than the enemy's false gospel. God's Word is creative, producing after itself in our lives. The enemy, however, *cannot* create, because he doesn't have that power. He can only destroy, by bringing poverty, sickness, disease and death.

According to Luke 9:1, Jesus called His 12 disciples together "and gave them power and authority" to cure diseases and drive out demons. We have that same authority over the works of darkness. But too often our confession lines up with what the enemy is doing to attack us rather than with what the Word has done to set us free from sickness.

We must always remember that the authority that God gives us through the Holy Spirit within us provides power over Satan and gives us the final say in our situation! The only way the enemy can affect us with symptoms is if we give him permission to do so. Are you giving him permission? Is your confession lining up with the enemy's symptoms? Or are your words and beliefs aligned with the Word of God?

The Root Cause of Sickness

While we often get caught up in symptoms, for most of us the real problem we have to deal with isn't the symptoms at all but the root of the sickness.

Every symptom has a root (otherwise it wouldn't be a symptom). If we only deal with the symptoms, we cover up the root. As long as the root of sickness still exists, the devil can make us sick again, even if we've already been healed. This is why God looks for transformation in our lives, not just quick fixes. So often we're looking for just a single, swift manifestation, but God wants to transform us so that we can be completely freed from the root of the problem and can continue to be a demonstration of His power to others.

There's a direct correlation between the symptoms of sickness in the Body of Christ and the condition of the Body as a whole. In other words, if a few segments of the Church are experiencing high levels of sickness, chances are good that people in those areas either don't know or don't understand the provision Christ made to bring healing to the world.

John 8:32 says, "And you will know the truth, and the truth will make you free." It's the truth *we know* that sets us free. Too many Christians don't seek out the full truth and don't truly study what God's Word says on a topic. When we take the time to study the subject of healing and wellness, we gain an understanding that there are root issues that we need to deal with first—issues that will continue to bring sickness and symptoms into our lives until we face them and allow Christ to transform them.

How do we experience this transformation? By turning our main attention to the Healer, not the healing. The closer we get to God, the further we get from our enemy. Rather than worrying about the symptoms, we need to turn our focus on God. We need to consistently mediate upon His Word, commune with Him in prayer and bask in His presence. When He captures our heart, His will becomes our desire, which in turn will deliver us from every symptom.

Any symptom of sickness (just like any symptom of sin) always indicates that we need more of God. We must pursue God until we learn how to purge all sin and sickness from our life.

When we question God by asking, "Why haven't You healed me?" we bypass the cross. God might respond to us with something like, "The question isn't whether *I've* done enough but whether *you've* done enough. What more do you want Me to do? Have I not sent My Son to the cross to deliver you?"

In past healing movements, a healing evangelist would come into a city or community, do a one- or two-day crusade and minister healing under the unction of the Holy Spirit. But once the evangelist left town, the anointing also left. The problem was that the healing evangelist could only deal with the symptoms of sickness, not the root of sickness.

For instance, an alcoholic suffering from liver failure might go to a healing crusade, believe God and receive a healed liver. However, if the issue of *drinking* is not dealt with, then the likelihood of the alcoholic once again experiencing liver problems is high.

When we opened the Healing Rooms, we recognized the need to deal with the root of infirmity, so we began to teach people—through a booklet called *How to Minister to Specific Diseases*—about how to both receive *and keep* their healing.

I want to share a few illustrations of diseases and their probable root causes, based on empirical evidence that we have observed in the Healing Rooms.

Fibromyalgia is an autoimmune deficiency disorder that is most commonly found in women. In our experience, women who are particularly prone are often those who have lost their headship. For instance, a woman's husband might leave her, and then she's left with responsibilities she finds difficult to handle: She has to raise the children, go to work and provide an income for the family. Because of this abandonment, she may harbor in her heart a lack of forgiveness against her husband. In my observations over the years, this lack of forgiveness eventually reveals itself as a root of bitterness. That bitterness begins to impact the body, causing weakness and pain in the woman's muscles and tissues. This, in turn, seems to lead to fibromyalgia.

The key we have found to healing from fibromyalgia is to deal with its root of unforgiveness and bitterness. The woman must forgive the man who left her. She also needs to ask the Lord to forgive her for taking onto herself what she should have given to Jesus—her bitterness and anger. As she releases the person for whom she carried pent-up resentment, she then begins to put an axe to the root of her affliction.

Every tree grows from a root. By no longer harboring a lack of forgiveness, the woman is simply cutting out the root of what I believe creates and sustains fibromyalgia.

Arthritis is fairly widespread, and one of the most commonly heard about is osteoarthritis, a degenerative condition that breaks down the joints. In my observation, it is often found in older people who tend to be perfectionists and frequently take on the spiritual, emotional and psychological burdens of the entire family. Often they are worriers, always fretting about their kids or grandkids and trying to keep the younger people from getting into things they shouldn't be doing. These worriers take on the whole weight of those burdens instead of casting their cares on Jesus.

According to our experience over the years, the root problem of osteoarthritis is taking on more than a person can handle. Dealing with this root issue requires that the person realize that *he* or *she* is not the burden bearer; Christ is. He said, "Take My yoke upon you and learn from Me, for I am gentle and humble in heart, and you will find rest for your souls. For My yoke is easy and My burden is light" (Matthew 11:29-30).

We need to ask the Lord to forgive us for carrying those things that we should be giving to Him. We need to transfer our load onto Jesus and begin to trust Him for the answer.

The other type of arthritis is similar to fibromyalgia and seems to stem from unforgiveness toward another person. Lack of forgiveness can result from many situations. Perhaps a person was due a promotion and then found out that it was given to someone else who had stepped on a lot of people in order to climb the corporate ladder. Or maybe a wife committed adultery, and her husband can't shake the image of betrayal. Or possibly a child died prematurely because of an accident or disease, and the parents' anger and unforgiveness has been directed toward God.

When we can't or won't release forgiveness toward whoever we feel has hurt us, it seems that this root of unforgiveness is able to produce inflammation of the joints. That's why it's imperative to forgive, no matter what.

Again, this is why many people who come to the Healing Rooms do not experience immediate manifestation of their healing: First they must acknowledge that there is a root that needs to be examined, and then they must allow God's healing balm to be applied to their hearts and minds so that the affliction—in this case arthritis—can finally be dealt with.

Depression seems to be affecting a growing number of people, and I have observed myriad root issues that can cause depression, or despair, to set in. Let me share just two examples.

A number of years ago we held a conference in London. At the end of the meeting, a lady came up for ministering, but she wouldn't look at me. She was very dejected and only looked down at the floor. I asked her what she wanted prayer for and she said, "I need prayer for healing and deliverance." I reached out to touch her to minister to her, and her eyes rolled back in her head and she slumped to the floor!

I sensed by the Holy Spirit that she needed some additional ministry, so a couple of team members and I took her aside and began to talk to her. We soon discovered that when she was a young girl, her father had been a gambler. Every week he would have men come over to the house to gamble—and the winner would get *her*. She hated her father and was so hurt and injured by those years of abuse. "I won't even allow a man to touch me," she said. I was then led by the Holy Spirit to tell her that what she needed was to forgive her father and, in turn, receive the blessing of her heavenly Father. She had an "orphan spirit," and she needed to receive the spirit of adoption.

I then asked her if I could give her a hug as a father and just bless her. "You can hug me if you want," she said, "but it won't make a bit of difference to me." That's when I really began to pray under my breath, "Holy Spirit, let me know exactly what this dear lady needs." As I prayed, the Holy Spirit told me to tell her that He would send a man across an ocean just for her. So I shared this with the young lady as I put my arms around her and began to bless her with the Father's blessing that she had never experienced before. As I was obedient to the Holy Spirit, I saw a tear come to the corner of her eye. She began to weep, and a lifetime of oppression and depression flooded out of her as she received the blessing of the Father for the first time in her life. It was that blessing that took away all the depression, hurt and anger that had been rooted within her.

I'll never forget the next night when I ministered. The woman walked alongside me and asked shyly if I could be her father. "Of course!" I responded. (I've got kids all over the world—some older than me. I don't know how that works, but I like it.) God did a wonderful work in that dear lady's life.

When the light of the Father falls onto the root issue, as it did with that woman, everything that has been covered up and causing failure in our lives is exposed. When we minister to those who are sick, though, we must remember that the only way we can properly and effectively get at the root cause is to ask the Holy Spirit to lead us—we only know in part, but He knows the whole situation.

One day, an elderly gentleman, probably in his early 80s, came to the Healing Rooms. He signed in for prayer and then sat down in the waiting room. The team members always take each sign-in sheet to their room and pray over the sheet first, asking the Holy Spirit to reveal what needs to take place. As they were praying over this man's sheet, they noticed the man had written on his sheet "A lifetime of depression." One of the men on the team got a mental image of a little sailboat. That picture stayed with him, so he knew the Holy Spirit was guiding him to go in that direction.

When the right time came, the team brought the elderly man into a room and introduced themselves.

The team member who had seen the sailboat said, "Sir, the Holy Spirit has given me a picture of a little sailboat. Can you tell me about it?"

The elderly man began to cry. As he wept, he shared a story about when he was a little boy. His family had lived on a farm that had a pond, and the man had made himself a little sailboat, which he loved to sail on the water.

He said, "I got up one morning and I had my sailboat on the table, because I was planning to go out and sail it after breakfast. But I said something that angered my grandfather so much that he picked up my sailboat and smashed it against the wall. Then he had a heart attack and died right before my eyes. I've blamed myself my entire life for the death of my grandfather. That's when my depression started."

Only by the Holy Spirit could we have known to ask that question. As the team ministered to him, he began to forgive himself and realize that his grandfather's death wasn't his fault. The lifetime of depression that had plagued this dear man began to leave, and he was set free from the devastation that the enemy had created in the man's life.

PRAYING FOR THE SICK

The Holy Spirit has distributed to every believer gifts to be used for furthering His kingdom on Earth. Those gifts include three that we call the "power gifts." They are (1) faith, (2) healing, and (3) working of miracles.

These power gifts are given to us for the benefit of the sick and are distributed by the Holy Spirit as He wills (see 1 Corinthians 12:4-11). The Holy Spirit always wills to fulfill the will of the Father, which is that none should perish but that all should come to repentance. As believers, it is our responsibility to yield to the power of the Holy Spirit in us to bring forth these gifts so that the will of the Father can be fulfilled through us. The gifts belong to God, but if we don't believe that we actually possess and can use the gifts—that we can pray for the sick—then we won't put these gifts into operation.

If we are on the street ministering to the lost and somebody needs a healing, we do not need to say to that person, "Wait here while I go get a healing evangelist. I can't pray for your healing because I don't have that particular gift." It's important that we know that there is a provision of healing in the atonement. We can "lay hands on the sick, and they will recover" (Mark 16:18).

Luke 10:19 says, "Behold, I have given you authority." Because we have the authority, it is our responsibility. It is improper for a Christian to say, "God, You heal them," because God has already said that *we* have authority on Earth, and that signs—including laying hands on the sick and they shall recover—will follow (see Mark 16:17-18).

There was a transfer of authority from God to Jesus, and then after His resurrection, Jesus transferred the authority to us:

And Jesus came up and spoke to them, saying, "All authority has been given to Me in heaven and on earth.

Go therefore and make disciples of all the nations, baptizing them in the name of the Father and the Son and the Holy Spirit, teaching them to observe all that I commanded you; and lo, I am with you always, even to the end of the age" (Matthew 28:18-20).

Jesus transferred His authority to His Body, the Church. As Ephesians 1:22-23 says, "He put all things in subjection under His feet, and gave Him as head over all things to the church, which is His body, the fullness of Him who fills all in all."

Even before His resurrection, Jesus gave us this responsibility:

Therefore I say to you, *all* things for which you pray and ask, believe that you have received them, and they will be granted you (Mark 11:24, emphasis added).

Scripture puts the responsibility for answered prayer on *us*. It's up to us to ask and to believe that we have received the answer. I think in this hour Jesus is looking down at His Body and saying something like, "This isn't what I had in mind. My Body is not supposed to be sick, because I made a provision at the cross for it to be well."

We need to realize that we have a greater dispensation for healing today than there was when Jesus was walking on the earth. I used to think that I would have loved to be here when Jesus was walking on the earth so that I could listen to His teaching and witness His miracles. But as I grew in the Lord, I began to fully understand the importance of Jesus returning to His Father, for He said, "It is to your advantage that I go away;

for if I do not go away, the Helper will not come to you; but if I go, I will send Him to you" (John 16:7).

With the presence of the Holy Spirit came the ability to perform greater miracles, as described by Jesus:

> Truly, truly, I say to you, he who believes in Me, the works that I do, he will do also; and greater works than these will he do; because I go to the Father (John 14:12).

As the Scriptures indicate, there is a greater authority in the Body of Christ now because we have Jesus sitting at the right hand of the Father, interceding for us, and the same Holy Spirit who raised Jesus from the dead dwells in us today.

As a man, Jesus could only be in one place at a time. He was subject to the same physical limitations that we are. But with the advent of the Holy Spirit's indwelling, the power of God who dwells in us now spreads like unquenchable fire throughout the earth. That's why God's Word knows no space boundaries or time limits. Even when we're unable to be near or even in the same vicinity as a loved one or an acquaintance in need of healing, we can speak forth the *rhema* word, and it will travel through spiritual time (which is timeless) to the person in need of a touch from the Lord, just as Jesus did for the child of the centurion in Matthew 8:5-13, confirming what Psalm 107:20 says: "He sent His word and healed them, and delivered them from their destructions."

Too many Christians today are afraid to pray for healing because they are worried about what might *not* happen. *What if I don't get healed—what will I do then?* What we do then is keep in mind that healing is not our responsibility; it's God's alone. It's our prayer but *His* power.

Healing is only difficult when we think we have something to do with it. When we leave it up to God, it's easy. So rather than worry about what we'll do if healing doesn't happen, we are to think about what we'll do when it *does*! It's God's Word, power and reputation on the line, not ours. The marvelous reality is that He honors His Word above His name, so He will perform what He said He would (see Psalm 138:2).

It is in exercising our faith and the anointing of the Holy Spirit within us that we become stronger. Everyone—every believer—can lay hands on the sick.

Every day our team members pray for the sick in Healing Rooms all over the world, and they witness greater and greater power as they exercise the anointing and watch God move in the lives of the hurting and the sick. We have people who come to us and want to become part of our ministry team, even though they think they don't have anything to offer. But my response to them is, "You're the one we're looking for. As long as you offer Jesus, you'll be fine."

That's the key: We are to just offer Jesus! We can lay hands on the sick and they shall recover because of the Holy Spirit. The key to getting the sick healed is not in what we possess but in *who* possesses us!

3

Healing
IS IN GOD'S
KINGDOM

LIVING IN RELATIONSHIP WITH GOD

Many people believe Christianity is nothing more than religion—a purposeless examination of God, looking at cold hard facts about Him without ever becoming intimately acquainted with Him. True Christianity is more than this. It is relationship with God, because the things God has in store for us do not come through examination and observation alone. If pursuing God is not done in the context of relationship, then it's an empty pursuit—it's mere religion.

For 25 years, I attended Bethel Church in Redding, California. During my time at Bethel, where I was a board member and an elder, I used to tell people I was the most bored member of the church. I felt like I was in a dry and thirsty land. The reason was because I had lived in *form* as a Christian but not in *power* as one. I had a life that was all neatly laid out, but it wasn't vibrant.

And for those 25 years, I plodded forward, thinking that God was going to come and just *fix* me.

Then revival came, and I realized that God wasn't coming to fix me—He was coming to kill me! He told me, "I don't want to 'fix' you, because I don't want you to be the way you are. I want you the way *I* am."

The apostle Paul tells us in Galatians 2:20, "It is no longer I who live." If I'm not the "I" who lives, then who is? Christ, who lives in me. It makes sense that someone has to "die" so that Someone better can live in me. We each need to "die"—that is, our natural, carnal nature must be suppressed so that Christ can take residence and live within us. It's simple: We can't have relationship with God when we're living *our* life rather than *His* life.

Having just a little bit of the gospel can make us miserable. Following Christ is an all-or-nothing proposal. As humans, we have to be trained in what it means to have a relationship with God.

Jesus said in Matthew 22:37-38, "'You shall love the Lord your God with all your heart, and with all your soul, and with all your mind.' This is the great and foremost commandment." Our relationship with God is to be set in love; we are to love His life more than we love our own. We do that by showing love outwardly, as an *action*.

We can't expect to receive something from God if we don't have relationship with Him. And a relationship with Him requires that our focus be on Him. If we're not focusing on God, then we're focusing on ourselves. And if we're focusing on ourselves, then we're focusing on the flesh—which leads to death.

We can't be *both* fleshly focused *and* God centered. We must be one or the other. The Lord has laid before us a choice between life (living His way) or death (ignoring His way). He even told us the correct choice to make: "Choose life" (Deuteronomy 30:19).

Life in God comes only through relationship with God. First John 2:15 says, "Do not love the world nor the things in the world." When you have a relationship with God, you won't have a relationship with the world that challenges or displaces God. True life comes as a result of living out the things of God rather than living as the god of things.

Too many people today are seeking God's *hand* rather than seeking His *face*. They treat Him like a genie in a lamp. They desire His help, perhaps even His companionship at times, but not the close intimacy of His presence.

ASSUMING DOMINION

For healing to occur in God's kingdom, the Body of Christ needs to move in dominion. "Dominion" means *absolute ownership*, *supreme authority* or *sovereignty*. That was what humans had with God in the beginning:

> Then God said, "Let us make man in our image, in our likeness, and let them rule over the fish of the sea and the birds of the air, over the livestock, over all the earth, and over all the creatures that move along the ground. Fill the earth and subdue it" (Genesis 1:26,28, *NIV*).

When Adam fell, he didn't lose heaven; he lost Earth. Through sin, he lost his God-given dominion over the planet. The redemption of humankind by Jesus Christ reinstalled that dominion and restored the authority Adam lost through his deliberate choice to sin:

> Christ redeemed us from the curse of the law by becoming a curse for us, for it is written: "Cursed is everyone who is hung on a tree." He redeemed us in order that the blessing given to Abraham might come to the Gentiles through Christ Jesus, so that by faith we might receive the promise of the Spirit (Galatians 3:13-14, *NIV*).

We've been redeemed from the curse so that we might receive the promise and the authority that was lost and that resulted in our sinful state. Christ Himself told us that He has given us authority "to overcome all the power of the enemy" (Luke 10:19). And the apostle Paul added, "Sin shall not be your master, because you are not under law but under grace" (Romans 6:14).

It's easy for most Christians to believe that if God Himself came down to lay hands on the sick, they would be healed. But why do these same Christians ignore the fact that *we* have been given that same power and authority? No wonder when we lay hands on the sick they are not healed!

When we begin to move in the authority and dominion God has given us, we will lay hands on the sick and *know* that they shall recover (see Mark 16:18). The Bible doesn't say the sick *might* recover; it says they *shall*.

THE REALITY OF THE UNSEEN

Reality is not limited to the natural realm of things we see. Reality goes far beyond what is merely seen with the eyes.

Remember, the natural realm is an *expression* of the supernatural realm. The unseen God existed before anything else; at His word, the seen came to be.

Today, we know of the existence of things that went unseen for thousands of years, including microorganisms, cells, molecules and atoms. Based on our expanded knowledge, reason tells us that spiritual reality includes the unseen. With the universe as vast as it is, there's no telling what else exists beyond our ability to see far into the deep reaches of space.

In fact, the unseen may be more real than what we can see. For example, Rembrandt was "more real" than the paintings he created, which are all we can see of his existence. In a similar way, God is "more real" than His created order. His creation is simply physical evidence of the supernatural reality behind it all. It is in that supernatural reality that true purpose, meaning and eternity are found. That is why if we're going to move in healing and miracles, we need to learn to move in the unseen spiritual realm.

What we see and call reality in this realm is only an expression of a greater reality that comes from the heavenly realm. "Out there" beyond us finite creatures here on Earth, a greater reality exists—all for the sole purpose of fulfilling God's plan. Therefore, we ought to "fix our eyes not on what is seen, but on what is unseen. For what is seen is temporary, but what is unseen is eternal" (2 Corinthians 4:18, *NIV*).

While all truth and meaning is contained in this unseen realm, God still loves His created order, the seen realm. He desires that we manifest His power in this realm—to transfer unseen truths from the supernatural realm to the natural.

Healing doesn't come through a form, a process, a procedure or anything that people do. It comes from the power of our (unseen) God having His will fulfilled through (seen) people walking in obedience to Him. God's will for healing His people is to be seen on the earth. He wants His will to be visible in the world through seen vessels (you and me) by the laying on of hands so that the sick might recover. This is the purest manifestation of the existence of the love of God for His people on Earth.

When we understand how to move in that unseen realm of reality, we will walk in it with a demonstration of the power of the Holy Sprit inside of us that reveals and fulfills God's will (see 1 Corinthians 2:4-5).

A Revival of Signs and Wonders

These signs will accompany those who have believed: in My name they will cast out demons, they will speak with new tongues; they will pick up serpents, and if they drink any deadly poison, it will not hurt them; they will lay hands on the sick, and they will recover. . . . And they went out and preached everywhere, while the Lord worked with them, and confirmed the word by the signs that followed (Mark 16:17-20).

Signs confirm God's Word to a lost world, showing people that Jesus is real and that God has a truth that will set them free. The world is looking for these signs in *this* hour—not somewhere off in the future.

A friend of mine, Bill Johnson, says, "You only need signs for a road that is not familiar." For nonbelievers, the road to God is unfamiliar; they need signs that point to Jesus. But the spirit of religion won't give signs, because it wants people to believe they've already arrived at their destination.

In Mark 16, when Jesus talked about the signs that would accompany believers, He raised the bar for "normal." What had been considered abnormal became the new normal. Signs and wonders became a standard expression of Christian ministry from Jesus through the first century. Unfortunately, too many people today have brought the Kingdom message back down to the level of what's normal by the world's standards.

If you're looking around for miracles in order to believe that there's a signs-and-wonders revival, then you're walking by sight rather than by faith. Sight looks for it and says, "It isn't here." Faith confesses it so that it will appear.

We have to believe that God is a God of miracles and that He wants to release all that He has into this realm.

"For as he thinks in his heart, so is he" (Proverbs 23:7, *NKJV*). We become what we think. In other words, thought creates. The mind that is set on the Spirit of God will be renewed with an understanding that God demonstrates what He creates through signs, wonders and miracles.

How do we establish a signs-and-wonders revival? We activate the creative will of God. We meet the condition of the Word. We stop trying to see miracles, and we *start confessing and proclaiming* them. Miracles are given to us by the Holy Spirit in order to reorder a disordered world. We are to *put on the miraculous!* It's part of the armor of God (see Ephesians 6:13-17; see also Isaiah 11:1-5 and 1 Corinthians 12:7-11).

THE WORKING OF MIRACLES

One of the gifts of the Spirit is the working of miracles (see 1 Corinthians 12:10). A miracle is simply an expression of God's creative will for us. It's no challenge for Him to bring a miracle into someone's life—He dwells in the miraculous. The miracle of healing, the gift of faith—all of the gifts that God gives us— are from His desire to restore His children to Him so that they can share His ways and wonders.

My friend Bill Johnson says, "A miracle isn't an encounter with what God does. A miracle is an encounter with who God *is*."

When we encounter the supernatural realm, we *should* see miracles! We begin to live in expectation of the miraculous. We begin to pray for miracles to be made manifest. We begin to call out for the miraculous.

At our ministry, we received a message from a prophet that the year 2006 was going to be a year of miracles. When the year began, staff and team members at our Healing Rooms Ministries corporate headquarters in Spokane fasted for 40 days in various ways. As we prayed throughout the year, we began to sense that God was going to work miracles.

In September 2006, we held our eighth annual Spiritual Hunger Conference. I didn't know exactly how it was going to happen, but I felt that miracles would come forth. On Saturday afternoon of the conference, I gave a message titled "God's Will for Miracles." At the end of my message, I felt the Holy Spirit saying, "Call people up who are missing limbs or who have body parts that have been removed, and we're going to call for the body parts to come into being."

Sixty to 70 people came forward. As they stood up front, I felt that we were going to see fingers and hands actually growing out. I requested that the audience begin to proclaim that the body parts grow. We had seen a vision of body parts in heaven. I had seen cubicles in heaven that went upward, clear out of sight. As graphic as it sounds, there were body parts in each of these cubicles. I sensed that God was ready to open the cubicles and start dispensing body parts.

As we began to proclaim the miracle, a lady in front of me started shouting and jumping around. *Wow*, I thought, *something is happening!* (With experience, you learn that every time you get an idea of what you think God is going to do, He goes beyond that and blows away your expectations.)

The lady who was shouting had previously had a double mastectomy. All the muscle and breast tissue had been removed, and the doctor said she would never again have any feeling or sensation in that area. When I began to pray for healing, this part of the body wasn't even on my radar. Nevertheless, this lady's muscles in the damaged area began to grow. She could feel them changing. As she continued to jump and shout, other ladies gathered around and watched as the woman's muscles began to regenerate. We couldn't help but glorify God for what He was doing.

A week after the conference, we got an email from that woman. Her breast muscles and tissue were continuing to develop, and even the scar from the original surgery was disappearing. In 2007, this lady came to our Spiritual Hunger Conference and shared what had happened since. She went back to the doctor who had performed the mastectomy for a follow-up exam. The doctor was amazed to see the new breasts and asked, "Who did this?"

Religion teaches us that because you cannot see it, it isn't there. Revelation teaches us that because we can't see it, it *is* there. Jesus said, "The kingdom of God is at hand"; therefore, it is reachable (Mark 1:15; see also Luke 10:9,11; 21:31). What is unseen in the kingdom of God *can* be reached by you and me. Therefore, a miracle isn't out of our reach; it is only out of our sight. We can confess those things that are not as though they are (see Romans 4:17). Remember, the existence of what you don't see is greater than the existence of what you do see. A miracle is simply a physical encounter with the creative will of God, brought forth by our unshakable faith in God.

> Therefore He who supplies the Spirit to you and works miracles among you, does He do it by the works of the law, or by the hearing of faith? (Galatians 3:5, *NKJV*).

It's impossible to walk on water when we sit in the boat and believe that even if Jesus Himself tells us to walk on water, we can't do it. If we don't believe, we will never achieve. If Peter had refused when Jesus said, "Come!" in Matthew 14:29, then Peter would not have stepped off of the seen and into the unseen and walked on the surface of the Sea of Galilee.

Remember, when the disciples were crossing the sea in the boat, the sea was stormy and the boat was being "battered by waves" (Matthew 14:24). Jesus told Peter to ignore the storm and tossing waves swirling around them, to trust Him and to do what He instructed. And Peter did so . . . and what stories he had to tell his children (if he had them)! How many people throughout history can begin a story with, "Let me tell you about the day I walked on the water with Jesus"?

It is our faith that allows us to trust God and move in the miraculous. To move in the miraculous, we cannot sit in the boat; we have to *do* something. We have to acquire an expectation that when people come to us with sickness, despair, addiction, broken relationships and even missing body parts, we can call forth a miracle into being.

With the mind of Christ, we believe that all things are possible. The greatest miracle in the end-time Church isn't going to be when a hand grows out; rather, it will be when the Body of Christ moves in absolute faith-filled authority. Colossians 2:9-10 says, "For in Him all the fullness of Deity dwells in bodily form, and in Him you have been made complete." If we've been made complete in Him and we're His body, then we are the temple of God and the Holy Spirit dwells in us. Therefore, we have a right to live *complete* lives—not missing anything that the enemy has stolen. Not even a body part.

If we try to proclaim a miracle by what we see in the natural, nothing will happen. We must see what's not yet in the natural—that which exists in the unseen realm—so that these unseen things can be released into this realm.

In Matthew 10:7-8, Jesus says, "As you go, preach, saying, 'The kingdom of heaven is at hand.' Heal the sick, raise the dead, cleanse the lepers, cast out demons. Freely you received, freely give." We have been freely given access to God's kingdom power. There's no need to wait or hesitate—it is already established. We need only to bring it forth. We don't need to pray for a movement in the miraculous—we need to start *becoming* a movement in the miraculous.

FOUR KINDS OF MIRACLES

There are four types of miracles in which to work:

1. *Diverse miracles.* Scripture promises us that various miracles are available to us *according to the will of God.* Hebrews 2:4 says, "God also testifying with them, both by signs and wonders and by various miracles and by gifts of the Holy Spirit according to His own will." In other words, God is saying that it is His will that by the power of the Holy Spirit within us, we have signs and wonders—that various miracles will take place to bear witness to Jesus working through us.

2. *Great miracles.* When the presence of God comes and His glory enters our midst, a capacity for great miracles, signs and wonders comes into being. Acts 6:8 says, "Now Stephen, a man full of God's grace and power, did great wonders and miraculous signs among the people" (*NIV*).

3. *Notable miracles.* Notable miracles are miracles that are well known—word of them spreads and their occurrence becomes common knowledge. A notable miracle is one that makes people sit up and take notice.

Acts 4:16 says, "What shall we do with these men? For the fact that a noteworthy miracle has taken place through them is apparent to all who live in Jerusalem, and we cannot deny it." Perhaps a Christian prays and a missing hand grows out, a well-known person is raised from the dead, a paraplegic receives the ability to walk or a person in a coma for years suddenly awakes; maybe a Christian prays and in the presence of medical professionals a tumor or a disease is completely healed; or maybe a Christian prays and a city receives a very public miracle that becomes a sign to all of who God is—these are all notable miracles.

4. *Unusual or special miracles.* Acts 19:11-12 says, "God was performing extraordinary miracles by the hands of Paul, so that handkerchiefs or aprons were even carried from his body to the sick, and the diseases left them and the evil spirits went out." In this case, miracles were actually transferred from Paul's body to cloth and from cloth to the sick, who were healed. We have seen demonstrations of this kind when there was an anointing on a cloth sent out to the sick, and the people were healed.

Not long ago, the Healing Rooms received a wonderful testimony from South Africa. A little girl had a brain tumor so severe that it was distorting her skull. She was in terrible pain and could not be moved. Her parents had heard about prayer cloths, so they contacted the Healing Rooms in South

Africa to inquire if they would send one on behalf of the child.

Our team in South Africa prayed over a prayer cloth and prepared to send it in the mail. However, they had some concern because the mail in South Africa doesn't always move very efficiently. So the Holy Spirit instructed them to anoint the cloth, pray over it and then make a copy of it on a photocopier and *fax* the copy to the parents! The parents took the faxed copy of the prayer cloth and tied it onto the head of their little girl. She broke out in a sweat for three days, and the tumor disappeared. That is the powerful (and, in this case, unusually creative) miracle-working power of God!

We cannot limit God by assuming that He will only work how we think He will or how we think things should happen. Let God be God! Paul said that "God chose the foolish things of the world to shame the wise" (1 Corinthians 1:27, *NIV*). If we're going to work miracles, we've got to move by a faith that causes us to do what looks ridiculous in the natural so that God can do the miraculous in the supernatural. We are to approach God with unlimited creativity, with full knowledge that He is the God of miracles and desires to give us what He has.

UNDERSTANDING GOD'S KINGDOM COME

Jesus demonstrated the way in which we are to pray: "Your kingdom come. Your will be done, on earth as it is in heaven" (Matthew 6:10). In order for the Body of Christ to move in power and heal the sick, we must have an understanding of what Jesus meant when He talked about the kingdom of God: the kingdom that comes on Earth *as God's will is done.*

Jesus continued to pray, "Deliver us from the evil one. For yours is the kingdom and the power and the glory forever" (Matthew 6:13, *NIV*). In order for the Body of Christ to be delivered from the evil one, we must move in the power of that deliverance.

Jesus also reassured us that God already knows our basic earthly needs: "Your heavenly Father knows that you need all these things" (Matthew 6:32). But in the very next verse He said, "But seek first His kingdom and His righteousness, and all these things will be added to you" (Matthew 6:33). We must first seek the Kingdom—because *all we need* is already there.

Too many people in the Body of Christ know the King but lack His provision, because they're not aware that when they seek Him with all their heart and soul, His kingdom provides all they need to live life and to serve Him (see Deuteronomy 4:29 and 2 Peter 1:3).

Jesus was commissioned to bring the kingdom, and that's what He commissioned *us* to do, too (see Matthew 10:7-8; 28:20; John 14:12). Jesus said in Matthew 12:28, "If I cast out demons by the Spirit of God, then the kingdom of God has come upon you." Yes, the kingdom of God *has* come upon us to heal the sick, raise the dead and do signs, miracles and wonders!

The Mysteries of God's Kingdom

Jesus Himself clearly said that the mysteries of the kingdom are available to the believer:

> To you it has been granted to know the mysteries of the kingdom of heaven (Matthew 13:11).

People in the natural can't see these mysteries—they are *spiritually* discerned and released. People who get caught up in a religious spirit and walk by sight or by religious "laws" can't even begin to understand the Kingdom. It remains hidden from them. People who want to justify their powerless walk as the norm go so far as to claim that the Kingdom doesn't really exist. And then there are those who call us—those who move in the power and dominion of God's gifts—fanatics, heretics or apostate (though such accusations cannot be backed up by Scripture).

Matthew 13:19 says, "When anyone hears the word of the kingdom and does not understand it, the evil one comes and snatches away what has been sown in his heart." The concept of *understanding* the word of the Kingdom in this passage involves the concept of bearing fruit. Understanding God's Word means embracing it, believing it and acting on it. For God's Word to be understood, it must be fruitful. For it to be fruitful, it must become active. For it to become active, it must move from heaven to Earth and become evident in our daily lives.

> I have food to eat that you do not know about. My food is to do the will of Him who sent Me and to accomplish His work (John 4:32,34).

We could almost think of God's Word as having been given to us in pill form (what one might call "Gos-pills"). However, these pills (the Word of God) do us no good unless we ingest them—take them into our spirit. Their active ingredient (the Holy Spirit) increases our faith. God has done His part by giving us seed (His Word). Now we must plant the seed within ourselves and sow it into the rest of the world in order for the harvest to come.

The Humility of Children

To understand the kingdom of God, we have to "become like children" and have a spirit of humility, as Jesus said, according to both Matthew and Luke:

> Truly I say to you, unless you are converted and become like children, you will not enter the kingdom of heaven. Whoever then humbles himself as this child, he is the greatest in the kingdom of heaven (Matthew 18:3-4).

> Truly I say to you, whoever does not receive the kingdom of God like a child will not enter it at all (Luke 18:17).

We must receive and believe as children of God, trusting Him without question.

A Dwelling Place of Victory

The Kingdom is a dwelling place of victory. Romans 14:17 says that "the kingdom of God is not eating and drinking, but righteousness and peace and joy in the Holy Spirit." When we are Kingdom minded, we have righteousness. We are in right standing with Christ. When our heart and our eyes are on Jesus, we have peace and joy to strengthen us, because the joy of the Lord is our strength (see Nehemiah 8:10). In such a dwelling place, the world will not be able to move us; only God can. This condition of righteousness, peace and joy is Christ in us.

It's Christ in the Church. It's Christ in the believer as a temple of the Holy Spirit.

First Corinthians 4:20 says, "For the kingdom of God does not consist in words but in power." It consists of the Holy Spirit power that is within every believer. It is the very power of Christ's resurrection.

The victory is going to come when the Kingdom is ministered all around the globe. Then it will be delivered up as the Church begins to reign as the kingdom of God.

> For He rescued us from the domain of darkness, and transferred us to the kingdom of His beloved Son, in whom we have redemption, the forgiveness of sins (Colossians 1:13-14).

We have not only been delivered *from* darkness, but we have also been transferred *into* the kingdom of God. That's why our faith is a demonstration of God's power, as the apostle Paul said in 1 Corinthians 2:4-5. We have resurrection power to demonstrate to the world who Jesus is, who the Father is and what His will is. It must be demonstrated because it's a truth that requires visualization in order to bring it into the seen realm.

Ambassadors for the Kingdom

We are ambassadors, called to fulfill the work of the Kingdom:

> We are ambassadors for Christ, as though God were pleading through us: we implore you on Christ's behalf, be reconciled to God (2 Corinthians 5:20, *NKJV*).

An ambassador is a diplomat. An ambassador's provision is not in the kingdom where he has been sent to; it is from the kingdom he has been sent *from*.

Ambassadors have diplomatic immunity. That is, they are not subject to the laws of the realm in which they are sent. They are subject to the laws of the realm they are *from*. Therefore, as ambassadors of Christ, you and I are no longer subject to the law of sin and death of this world; we are subject to the law of our heavenly Kingdom (which contains *no* sickness or death).

Death to the Self

We only experience resurrection power when we die to the self and come alive in Jesus. Resurrection is repossession. When the Holy Spirit comes, life returns.

> I have been crucified with Christ; and it is no longer I who live, but Christ lives in me; and the life which I now live in the flesh I live by faith in the Son of God (Galatians 2:20).

We cannot move in resurrection power while continuing to cling to our own life, our own agenda. God is trying to separate us from fleshly desires that only lead to death (see Romans 8:6). To move in resurrection power, we must die in the flesh so that we can live in the Spirit. The flesh is shakable, but the kingdom of God cannot be shaken: "We are receiving a kingdom which cannot be shaken" (Hebrews 12:28, *NKJV*).

Humanity's problem is as much unbelief as it is sin. We must have an unshakable belief in our God and in His Word. If we truly, fully believe in and love God, then we will do as He says (see John 14:15). Only then can His kingdom come through us to heal the sick, cause limbs to grow out and bring miracles and signs into the Body of Christ and to the world. Then the world will know that our victory is just as much in the resurrection of Jesus as in the atonement brought by His death.

Jesus stated that His expelling demons and healing the sick were evidence that the kingdom of God has come upon the earth (see Matthew 12:28). He wasn't just bringing healing and miracles; He was bringing the kingdom.

The Rule of a Theocracy

Our problem today is that we have been raised in a republic of the people, by the people and for the people. We live in a democracy, where everyone has equal rights, each person can speak his or her own mind, and people can go wherever they want to go and do whatever they want to do within the bounds of the governing laws. In our free society, we have near total liberty of life—and that's the problem: in a fallen world, a democracy is necessary.

But God's kingdom is a theocracy, where the King rules. In the kingdom of God, we don't have a vote on how the rules are set; we must choose to obey the King. But the payoff is great: When we obey our King, all He has is made available to us as our inheritance.

In God's kingdom, we don't go until the Holy Spirit tells us when and where to go. We don't speak until the Holy Spirit tells us what to speak. Our democratic, majority-rules mindset makes it difficult for Christians to process this way of thinking.

Many people have a strained relationship with our Creator because they resist fully submitting in utter humility to another power. But with a purely democratic perspective, we will never be able to completely resist the kingdom of darkness. Complete resistance to the enemy only comes when we have a Kingdom perspective. We are to come to God and lay down our life for Him, and He will replace our life and our ways with His life and His ways.

This is a major problem for the Church in a culture like ours with a history of the democratic process and where many denominational systems lead Christians to believe that things should be done their way. God's kingdom is not some hamburger stand—you can't have it your way. It must always be God's way.

The greatest victory we believers can ever have is when we die to the self. Only then can Christ live in us. Then we have righteousness, peace and joy in the Holy Spirit. Then we can dwell in victory. No longer can the enemy move us. We will be moved only by God. And only then will the kingdom of God come to His children here on Earth as it is in heaven.

4

ROADBLOCKS TO

You get in the car and turn the key, and the engine rumbles to life. You shift into drive, check your mirrors, flip the turn signal, hit the gas and the motor roars . . . but the car doesn't budge. You give it more gas. The engine groans louder and the car shudders . . . but still no movement. Frantically, your mind races through a series of checklists regarding what may be wrong. Then you see that little lever, the one you never use, the one that was set in place by the last driver: the parking brake. The parking brake is set, blocking you from moving. But with a simple lowering of the handle, you are free to motor on down the road.

If we're going to receive something from God, then we must have a belief system that allows us to do so. It can be very discouraging when things in our life block our healing. Like the car with the parking brake set, we try to move forward but make no progress. If we're going to move in the power of God to see the sick healed, then we have to deal with things in life that block the move, no matter where the interference comes from.

There are eight roadblocks to God's healing, and in this chapter, we'll examine each one in turn:

1. Lack of forgiveness
2. Lack of knowledge
3. Sin in our lives
4. Lack of faith
5. Communion (improper discernment of the Lord's Body)
6. Unbelief
7. Being problem-centered
8. Justifying our condition rather than claiming our position

We'll also discuss a few frequently asked questions and a couple of problem Bible passages to dispel any lingering doubts about where we need to stand.

BLOCK #1: LACK OF FORGIVENESS

Scripture talks about us being mountain movers, about speaking truth and receiving what we ask for from God:

> Jesus answered saying to them, "Have faith in God. Truly I say to you, whoever says to this mountain, 'Be taken up and cast into the sea,' and does not doubt in his heart, but believes that what he says is going to happen, it will be granted him. Therefore I say to you, all things for which you pray and ask, believe that you have received them, and they shall be granted you" (Mark 11:22-24).

We lean on this verse when we want to receive physical or emotional healing. However, the condition we are in is determined by the position we take. Some people take a position that disregards the truth about healing. That is why some people ask, but they don't receive. As Jesus continues His teaching, He offers a possible explanation as to why this is:

> Whenever you stand praying, forgive, if you have anything against anyone, so that your Father also who is in heaven will also forgive you your transgressions. But if you do not forgive, neither will your Father who is in heaven forgive your transgressions (Mark 11:25-26).

We can't be set free if we're not willing to forgive those we're holding something against. That's why God set this as one of the conditions for those who wish to receive from Him.

God tells us that He gives grace to the humble but resists the proud (see Proverbs 3:34; see also James 4:6; 1 Peter 5:5). When we pray that we will receive whatever we ask for, one of the conditions is that we must first forgive everyone who has hurt or wronged us. If we don't, then try as we might, we can ask for a healing but we won't receive it, because we haven't met this condition for healing to flow. The parking brake is still set!

Why can't some people seem to forgive? Because they have a tendency to equate the sin with the sinner. We are to hate the sin only. Unfortunately, too many people haven't truly forgiven the sinner, because to them, the person has *become the sin* that was committed.

Some people use the excuse, "Well, you just don't know what they've done to me. They've injured me so badly I can't forgive them."

The truth is, it doesn't matter what they've done to us. What matters is that we are willing to do what God requires of us, no matter what someone has committed against us. We must forgive. We must learn to separate the sin from the sinner. That is what Jesus did for us—He bore our sins so that we wouldn't have to pay for them. He separated us from our sins so that we could be forgiven. He asks the same in response.

Healing requires us to be connected to God. Lack of forgiveness causes us to be separated from God. When we don't deal with an issue of lack of forgiveness, when we don't forgive everyone we've ever held any malice against, spiritual blockage cuts us off from God (see Block #3 below).

BLOCK #2: LACK OF KNOWLEDGE

The Bible tells us that "[God's] people are destroyed for lack of knowledge" (Hosea 4:6). This is because knowledge—intimate knowledge of God and His Word—brings with it God's power *and* produces faith. Knowledge increases power (see Proverbs 24:5). Lack of knowledge opens the door for the enemy to destroy us.

It is paramount that every believer has full knowledge of the will of God to heal us. We cannot move in faith if we don't have the Word in us to produce it.

The prophet Isaiah said:

Therefore my people have gone into captivity, because they have no knowledge; their honorable men are famished, and their multitude dried up with thirst. Therefore Sheol has enlarged itself and opened its mouth beyond measure; their glory and their multitude and their pomp, and he who is jubilant, shall descend into it (Isaiah 5:13-14, *NKJV*).

When we don't have knowledge, we fall into captivity, because without the truth of the Word of God concerning His will to heal us, the enemy can overwhelm us.

Psalm 111:10 says, "The fear of the LORD is the beginning of wisdom." You don't get the wisdom of God without getting the Word of God (His knowledge) into you. Wisdom is the proper application of God's knowledge. Wisdom shows us what to do with knowledge of His Word. It's what we do with this knowledge that determines where we can go in God.

For the LORD gives wisdom; from His mouth come knowledge and understanding (Proverbs 2:6).

The word "understanding" in this Scripture means *intelligence*. It is our capacity to learn from God. It's not enough to gain knowledge without an understanding of the knowledge. There must always be a link between the two. When the Holy Spirit brings understanding to us, He increases our ability to learn even more.

Proverbs 3:13 says, "How blessed is the man who finds wisdom and the man who gains understanding." Theologians may have much knowledge, but that knowledge will lack life if it is without an understanding brought by the Holy Spirit. When we find God, we find wisdom. When we apply wisdom to knowledge, we gain understanding. Understanding reveals why God gives us His Word: that we might fulfill His will on the earth.

BLOCK #3: SIN IN OUR LIVES

Sin that has not been dealt with will block the word of healing from coming to us. Sin cuts us off from God, as Isaiah 59:2 teaches:

> Your sins have cut you off from God. Because of sin he has turned his face away from you and will not listen anymore (*TLB*).

When we do things because we willfully lack knowledge or truth, or when we do know but we choose not to obey, that is sin. God resists the proud when they sin, because they are operating outside of His will. If we intend to partner with God but allow lust or greed or covetousness or any other kind of sin to remain unchecked in our lives, then we are asking God to partner with us in our sin. We want Him to bring us our healing *while* we are disobeying His Word *and* becoming an affront to Him by defiling ourselves. In effect, we are trying to join Him to our sin.

Not only do our own sins prevent us from receiving the things of God, but we can also suffer from the consequences of sins our ancestors engaged in. Generational sins of the past can have devastating effects on our own lives.

God holds fathers responsible for the spirituality of their family, as it says in Deuteronomy 5:9:

> I, the LORD your God, am a jealous God, visiting the iniquity of the fathers on the children, and on the third and the fourth generations of those who hate Me.

In cities across America, we see the consequences of the sins of fathers affecting their children. We see it in cities that have topless bars, drunkenness, drug use, prostitution and high crime rates—activities resulting from the sins of forefathers who initiated them. Subsequent generations must now dwell in the shadows of those sins and deal with their aftereffects. Even health issues such as asthma and many other physical and physiological infirmities are passed down through the generations.

Generational curses—curses that result from sin (see Deuteronomy 27:15-26) or curses that were spoken by an ancestor or that came upon an ancestor (see Joshua 6:26; 1 Kings 16:34)—can also come through an individual or through the corporate sin in a city where the people participate in destructive activities that prey on the poor and uneducated.

We all pay for (and must live with) the consequences of the sins of generations past, but we also have the ability to receive forgiveness for generational sins and to break generational curses (see Jeremiah 14:20; Daniel 9:8,20; 1 Peter 1:18; 1 John 1:9): Scripture tells us that we are not bound eternally by generational sins, because God shows mercy to all those who love Him and keep His commandments (see Deuteronomy 5:10). In addition, the power of the Holy Spirit in the believer is enough to break the strongholds of previous generations, as we are told in Galatians 3:13: "Christ redeemed us from the curse of the law" (see also 1 Peter 1:18-19).

BLOCK #4: LACK OF FAITH

"Without faith it is impossible to please Him, for he who comes to God must believe that He is and that He is a rewarder of those who seek Him" (Hebrews 11:6). Doubt created by improper understanding of the Word will prevent healing from taking place. Lack of faith from the people prevented Jesus from healing the sick in His own hometown when He laid hands on them:

> He could not do any miracles there, except lay his hands on a few sick people and heal them. And he was amazed at their lack of faith (Mark 6:5-6, *NIV*).

If faith is the substance of things hoped for (see Hebrews 11:1), then fear is the substance of things *not* hoped for.

It is faith that moves us into the things of God and gives us the power to overcome the plots of the enemy. Isaiah reminds us that God wants us to put our trust in Him: "The steadfast of mind You will keep in perfect peace, because he trusts in You" (Isaiah 26:3). When we face our God and have our being in Him, then He moves us rather than the enemy moving us.

Scripture is clear: If we lack faith, then we can't please God. And when we can't please God, we can't receive healing.

BLOCK #5: COMMUNION (IMPROPER DISCERNMENT OF THE LORD'S BODY)

Improper discernment of the Lord's Body—how we approach the Communion table—can affect our healing. Paul specifically addresses this issue in 1 Corinthians 11:27-29:

> Therefore whoever eats this bread or drinks this cup of the Lord in an unworthy manner will be guilty of the

body and blood of the Lord. But let a man examine himself, and so let him eat of that bread and drink of that cup. For he who eats and drinks in an unworthy manner eats and drinks judgment to himself, not discerning the Lord's body (*NKJV*).

The purpose of Communion is to remind us of and reaffirm in us the benefits of the Cross. According to Scripture, if we take the cup in an unworthy manner, we are cursed. If we don't rightly discern what is represented in the cup and in the bread, then we lose the benefit they represent: "For this reason many among you are weak and sick" (1 Corinthians 11:30).

Too many people in the Church today are weak and sick. Often, this is a result of a misunderstanding of Communion.

Communion is a representation of what Jesus provided on the cross for our ultimate healing. The cup represents the blood poured out for our sin. The bread represents His body broken for our curse. But when we take Communion in doubt or unbelief, we render its effect useless in our body, leaving us open to sickness and a drain on our power.

We should share in Communion as often as we can, not just to remember what Jesus has done for us, but also to have full access to all that His sacrifice represents for us, including knowing that His sacrifice has a medicinal quality for us. But to take it in the wrong way is to virtually swallow poison, because the curse comes off of Jesus and falls on a doubting person. Scripture is very clear about the fact that when we take Communion in an unworthy manner, we drink and eat damnation to ourselves, as Paul states in 1 Corinthians 11:29.

Hebrews 10:29 adds some insights on this subject:

How much more severely do you think a man deserves to be punished who has trampled the Son of God under foot, who has treated as an unholy thing the blood of the covenant that sanctified him, and who has insulted the Spirit of grace? (*NIV*).

This powerful Scripture addresses the issue of wrongly discerning what is represented in the Cross. The Father sent His Son to the cross to bear our sickness, to carry our pain on His body, so that we would be healed. When we don't cherish the truth of what Jesus provided on the cross, when we partake in Communion amidst doubt and unbelief, then we trample all over the Son of God. The word "trampled" in this verse means *rejected with disdain*. The word "grace" means *favor*. In effect, Scripture is saying that whoever scornfully rejects the Son of God deserves severe punishment because they have insulted God, lost His favor and cursed themselves by belittling Jesus' sacrifice on the cross.

So Jesus said to them, "Truly, truly, I say to you, unless you eat the flesh of the Son of Man and drink His blood, you have no life in yourselves. He who eats My flesh and drinks My blood has eternal life, and I will raise him up on the last day. For My flesh is true food, and My blood is true drink. He who eats My flesh and drinks My blood abides in Me, and I in him" (John 6:53-56).

When we take the cup representing Jesus' shed blood and the bread representing His broken body, we have His life in us, as the apostle Paul stated:

But if the Spirit of Him who raised Jesus from the dead dwells in you, He who raised Christ Jesus from the dead will also give life to your mortal bodies through His Spirit who dwells in you (Romans 8:11).

The word "life" refers to the process of quickening our mortal bodies with the life of Jesus. Communion is the powerful life force of Jesus, bringing healing to our body. Many of us need to come to the Lord and say, "Lord, forgive me for ever taking Your cup and Your body in an improper manner in the past." Then we need to receive Communion in the right way, believing that it is the life of Jesus.

BLOCK #6: UNBELIEF

Most people have experienced going to the doctor and being tested and checked for various ailments. Doctors are there to get us healed. They've made a commitment to bring healing to all who come to them. But too often people have a tendency to trust the doctor more than they trust God, the Great Physician. It's important that we rely more on God than the physician we go to in the natural.

My perspective from my experience in the Healing Rooms is that we need to go to the doctor in the natural realm until we learn how to go to Jesus in the spiritual realm. In other words, if we're trying to grow in God, then we need to go to a doctor until our faith is built up by the Word so that it can produce a manifestation of healing. The fact that we go to the doctor isn't going to stop God from fulfilling His will in us. Jesus is not going to say, "Well, I wanted to heal them, but they went to the doctor, so I guess they don't want My healing." In fact, if our doctor is treating us and we're also going to Jesus, and we experience a manifestation of healing, then our doctor will be happy because his job is finished (and he can still send us a bill!). But it is the work of God in our body that will become to all a testimony of the unexplainable healing power of Jesus.

Going to the doctor is okay and is often the wise thing to do. But if we can go to Jesus first and throughout the time we're being treated in the natural, then when we get healed, we can stop going to the doctor. In the meantime, we need to take our medicine and do what the doctor requires us to do until Jesus brings us our healing.

Never tell others that going to a doctor somehow means they lack faith. Telling people that they don't have enough faith brings condemnation. How can we encourage people when we've just discouraged them in a judgmental manner? We just need to keep in mind that we don't set our main trust in doctors but in the Lord, as the prophet Jeremiah tells us:

This is what the LORD says: "Cursed is the one who trusts in man, who depends on flesh for his strength and whose heart turns away from the LORD" (Jeremiah 17:5, *NIV*).

If we receive prayer and there is a beginning of healing in our body, it is important that we continue to go to the doctor and that we ask to be taken off our medication as soon as possible. The doctor can do an examination to make sure that the healing is actually taking place. As that process takes effect and the doctor tapers off the treatment, then we can praise God and give *Him* full credit.

BLOCK #7: BEING PROBLEM-CENTERED

Scripture says, "Submit yourselves, then, to God. Resist the devil, and he will flee from you" (James 4:7). Our enemy is supposed to be on the run, fleeing from us, under our feet (see Romans 16:20), because He who is in us is greater "than he who is in the world" (1 John 4:4).

There can be a struggle, however, between us and the devil, because the enemy wants us to face him so that he can cause us to walk by *his* vision of our circumstances rather than by our faith in God. When we walk by what we see and how we feel rather than by every word that comes from the mouth of God (see Matthew 4:4), we have a tendency to fear our enemy more than we fear our God.

Problem-centered people are usually more impacted by what the devil does than by what God does. By tending to relate more with the enemy than with God, they suffer from a crisis of identity. Eventually, they have a difficult time recognizing the enemy because he has become so familiar to them.

Either we're going to focus on our problems or we're going to focus on God and His solutions. We can't be problem-centered when we are God-centered.

BLOCK #8: JUSTIFYING OUR CONDITION RATHER THAN CLAIMING OUR POSITION

Believing that healing isn't for everyone is actually an attempt to justify our condition rather than claim our position. Nothing blocks the flow of healing as much as when we hesitate to fully believe that healing is for all people at all times.

> For God did not send the Son into the world to judge the world, but that the world might be saved through Him (John 3:17).

The word "saved" here literally means to be made whole. If salvation is for all, and Jesus came that we might be saved (be made whole), then that wholeness is for every person. Unfortunately, just as not every person will choose to be saved, likewise not every person will choose to be healed. However, that doesn't stop the provision of Jesus' sacrifice on the cross from being available to everyone.

Some people justify their unhealed condition by suggesting that they have been afflicted for God's glory. They sometimes point to such Scriptures as John 9:1-3:

> And as He passed by, He saw a man blind from birth. And His disciples asked Him, "Rabbi, who sinned, this man or his parents, that he would be born blind?" Jesus answered, "It was neither that this man sinned, nor his parents; but it was so that the works of God might be displayed in him."

It is illogical to think that *God* afflicts us for His glory, because the logical conclusion of that premise would lead one to think that in order to give God even more glory, we would have to get sicker. Of course, that thinking is ridiculous. God doesn't get the glory for what the devil does to make us sick. The glory to God comes when the person is *healed* of a malady, as was the case with the blind man in John 9. The work of God was displayed in the blind man's life when he was miraculously healed. Witnessing that kind of healing is what then draws the unsaved to the salvation of Jesus (see John 10:21).

Can you imagine a nonbeliever looking at a sick person and saying, "Wow! I want that"? Of course not. It is far more likely that a person will be attracted to Christianity by witnessing a miraculous healing.

Another mistake unhealed people make in justifying their condition is believing that they have been afflicted so that God might teach them some sort of lesson. Being sick or afflicted doesn't *teach* us anything. We must fully understand that faith does not come through sickness. The devil wants us to believe that we're sick. But God wants us to know that we're healed by the stripes of Jesus. And until that healing comes and relieves us of all suffering, we should not whine or complain. We should rejoice. Why? Because suffering produces perseverance; perseverance produces character; character produces hope; and hope never disappoints, because God loves us and wants us to be whole (see Romans 5:3-4).

Have you ever heard a Christian say, "I will be healed *if* it is God's will"? This kind of a statement is filled with doubt and reveals a lack of faith about God's desire that His children not be in sickness. God's will is that we are healed by the stripes of Jesus. He doesn't withhold that from us—indeed, He desires to demonstrate it to a watching world through us.

We must not justify what the enemy does—we are neither to ascribe it to God nor suggest that God withholds goodness from His obedient followers. That brings the Word down to the level of our experience rather than raise our experience to the level of the Word.

FREQUENTLY ASKED QUESTIONS

There are three important questions that I am frequently asked about healing in accordance with the Word of God.

1. If God Wants to Heal Us, Why Do We Die?

God does not promise us that we will not die. He tells us, "It is appointed for men to die once" (Hebrews 9:27). We will die, but it is God's desire that we will live whole lives that fully glorify God until we transfer to heaven.

Exodus says, "I will remove sickness from your midst. . . . I will fulfill the number of your days" (Exodus 23:25-26). The reason God takes sickness away is because He is Jehovah Rapha, a God of healing. He loves His children and desires us to be well. He wants our days fulfilled so that our destiny will be fulfilled. He wants to establish a relationship with us and to see us fulfill the Great Commission so that others might also enjoy that relationship with Him.

The psalmist cries, "O my God, do not take me away in the midst of my days" (Psalm 102:24). It is God's will that during our finite time here on Earth, we will live to declare His work in the world. Christians are not to become attached to the world or the things hereof, because our true home, our final home, is in heaven.

It is the enemy's will that we stop spreading God's Word, that we stop winning souls and that we live in distracting sickness. We are in a life-and-death battle with demonic powers here on Earth. In the war between good and evil, the goal of the devil is to take out the warrior and steal faith from Christians any way he can. As Paul told the Ephesians, this is the primary battle of the Christian life: "For our struggle is not against flesh and blood, but against the rulers, against the powers, against the world forces of this darkness, against the spiritual forces of wickedness in the heavenly places" (Ephesians 6:12).

2. What Happens When Someone Receives Prayer for Healing but the Symptoms Persist?

Too often, when we don't have an answer to our prayers, we think that either sin is blocking the healing or it's not God's will that the healing take place. But—and this bears repeating— *when we pursue healing, it is vitally important that we not rely on man but on God alone.* It's easy to seek out people to pray for us rather than to rely on the Word of God. Healing can come by the prayers of others, but there will always be something deposited in us when we are the doers of the Word. God's goal is to bring both a manifestation of healing in the physical and a revelation of spiritual knowledge from the healing.

God wants everyone to be impacted by all of Him. He wants to strengthen us in spirit, mind and body. If people need more faith, then we have a responsibility to give them God's Word on healing so that they can receive faith that produces results. If there is sin, we are to pray with them and let the Holy Spirit bring conviction. We are to stand firm in God and take up His whole armor. In that way, we will be able to withstand "in the evil day" (Ephesians 6:13). Hebrews 10:35-36 tells us to hang on to our confidence in the Lord and the promises of His Word:

> Therefore, do not throw away your confidence, which has a great reward. For you have need of endurance, so that when you have done the will of God, you may receive what was promised.

Our endurance is to be constant, not wavering no matter what. The enemy will fight to keep the symptoms before us so that we will begin to lose confidence. When we lose confidence, we lose endurance; when we lose endurance, we lose faith; when we lose faith, we lose the promise.

Our belief system will either focus on the symptom or on the Word of truth. One leaves us bound and captive; the other sets us free.

The symptoms of sickness don't determine whether or not we're healed. Only the Word does. The Word tells us: "By His stripes we are healed" (Isaiah 53:5, *NKJV*).

3. What About Paul's "Thorn in the Flesh" Mentioned in 2 Corinthians 12:7?

Some people think that the thorn in Paul's flesh describes a sickness that God refused to heal. This mindset believes that God sometimes keeps people in bondage. But 2 Corinthians

12:7 says, "A thorn in the flesh was given to me, a messenger of Satan to buffet me, lest I be exalted above measure" (*NKJV*). I believe that this Scripture indicates that the "messenger of Satan" was a person, not a thing. Paul says it was sent to "buffet" him—blow after blow, like the waves that would pound against a boat. The inference is that the thorn was not necessarily a sickness or disease, but rather some form of ongoing attack from the devil—something that was a constant vexation to Paul. But he realized that the grace of God was sufficient strength for him to bear up under the assault:

> Concerning this I implored the Lord three times that it might leave me. And He has said to me, "My grace is sufficient for you, for power is perfected in weakness." Most gladly, therefore, I will rather boast about my weaknesses, so that the power of Christ may dwell in me. Therefore I am well content with weaknesses, with insults, with distresses, with persecutions, with difficulties, for Christ's sake; for when I am weak, then I am strong (2 Corinthians 12:8-10).

It's only when the strength of God comes upon us that we have the power to overcome. When we are aware of our weakness, the power of God rests upon us.

It was the power of God that rested upon Paul and gave him the authority to overcome whatever the enemy was bringing against him. Everywhere Paul went, the devil stirred up trouble for him. Paul wrote of the many trying times when he had been whipped repeatedly, stoned, left for dead, thrown in jail and attacked by lions, among other things (see 2 Corinthians 11:24–27). In all of his writings of persecution and tribulations, though, not one time did he talk about this "thorn in the flesh" weakness or any kind of sickness. When he mentioned all the trials he went through, he didn't list a specific eye disease (see Galatians 6:11) or a speech impediment (see 2 Corinthians 10:10). If Paul himself didn't mention any sickness that he may or may not have been dealing with, then we should take this as an example for us not to dwell on such things. Such focus only indicates a lack of faith.

"Problem" Bible Passages

There are those who claim that there are passages in Scripture that seem to contradict the very issue of healing. One example is 2 Timothy 4:20, which describes Paul departing Miletus and leaving behind Trophimus, who was sick. Another example is 1 Timothy 5:23, which describes Timothy having a stomach condition for which Paul advised him to use wine to remedy. These two verses may cause some people to doubt that healing can happen all the time.

However, we have to be very careful how we interpret the way the early writers used the word "sick" or "sickness." The Greek word translated here as "sick" literally means "weak" or "without strength." We don't know the precise age or physical condition of Trophimus, but it is possible that Paul left him in the city because Trophimus had been traveling a lot and simply didn't have the strength to continue.

The fact that Paul left Trophimus in Miletus needn't cause us to doubt that Jesus is a healer. I believe that a recovery needed to take place—Trophimus needed to rest. No one can keep going and going with little rest. It's no different today. We can't do ministry without getting the proper rest; otherwise, we will have weakness and infirmity in our body and be useless in fulfilling His will.

Just as Trophimus suffered weakness, so did Timothy, and Paul advised Timothy to take wine for his stomach ailment. I believe Paul instructed Timothy to take some wine because Paul believed it would strengthen or heal Timothy's stomach. Sometimes people eat the wrong foods when they should eat healthy foods—which can overcome the effects of the bad foods. We can become weak if we eat something we shouldn't, and we might have to take something that contains a healing property that can overcome stomach problems that result from our poor eating. Paul might have been suggesting that wine is good to strengthen a weak stomach or one that is upset.

As believers, we have a responsibility to steward our bodies and take in the proper nutrients in order to maintain good health. If we put good things into our body, we get good results. If we put bad things in, we get bad results. We can't eat things that are bad for the body and then turn around and complain to God that we are sick and expect Him to fix us. If we've eaten something that has caused us to have a stomach ailment, then we may have to take something that will calm our stomach and bring it back into proper order.

There are many roadblocks to healing. We simply need to stand on Scripture, claim the promises contained in the Word of God, and pray for the naysayers and doubters. Our God can do *anything!*

5

GOD'S POWER, OUR Authority

When God sent my wife and me from Redding, California, to Spokane, Washington, I spent nearly a year and a half praying and seeking the reason why God chose to move us.

In Redding, there had been a great renewal movement of the Holy Spirit. But Spokane was much different. I'd heard from people many times that Christian leaders leave Spokane to go elsewhere because it's so difficult to be truly effective there. Also, I couldn't find anyplace where there was a real move of the Holy Spirit such as I had experienced in Redding. Month after month I prayed, pursuing God for an answer.

Finally, in my desperation, I remembered what Bill Johnson had told me about people who needed a breakthrough: They fasted for 40 days. *Forty days?!* I'd never even fasted for 4 hours, let alone 40 days. But I realized that I needed to do something on a whole new level, so I started fasting.

I quickly discovered that the fast was not for the purpose of moving and changing God—it was for moving and changing *me!* It was the only way I could hear from God. At the end of that 40-day fast, the Holy Spirit began to talk to me. He told me I would never walk on water if I was sitting in the boat. He told me there's a time to pray and a time to move—and *now* was the time to move. He wanted me to re-dig the generational wells of healing that John G. Lake had started in the city of Spokane, to re-open the well of healing, to call forth intercessors, to pray for the sick once again.

I tell you this story because it illustrates an important dynamic: the relationship between the body and the spirit. It takes that kind of perseverance and that kind of fast to make an exchange so that the Holy Spirit can begin to reveal things to us that we wouldn't have otherwise seen.

So often we're wrapped up in the flesh, so busy feeding our desires, that we neglect to feed our spirit . . . and then we miss what the *Spirit* (capital *S*) is trying to tell us. Only when we have the flesh in its proper place (subjected to the Spirit) are we able to possess true spiritual power and God's full anointing on our lives.

THE TEMPLE OF THE HOLY SPIRIT

"For the mind set on the flesh is death, but the mind set on the Spirit is life and peace" (Romans 8:6). When we focus on the flesh, we fail. Before we are saved, our natural inclination is to focus on our own desires. Our mind is "set on the flesh" instead of "on the Spirit." Our thoughts, our motives, our desires, our actions—all revolve around our flesh, around satisfying our body. But when we are born again, our mind is transformed to focus on the Spirit. It is then that we truly became a spiritual being—which is how God created us in the beginning.

God never intended for us to be led by the flesh, nor did He intend for us to be led by the mind. We were created to be far more than mere physical (or even mental) beings. We were created to be *spiritual* beings (see John 3:3,6). When we are born again, we become spiritually alive. That's why Paul says, "You are not in the flesh but in the Spirit, if indeed the Spirit of God dwells in you" (Romans 8:9).

Unfortunately, many Christians forget that once God redeems us and saves us, our flesh is no longer inherently evil. Our bodies become *vessels* that God works through to pour out His healing to the world. It is through *us*—our mouths, our hands, our feet, our prayers—that God brings healing and redemption to those who are lost and hurting in this world. Too often, Christians miss that point. They are consumed with a sin consciousness that forgets that they have been forgiven. They try to continue to live by the Law rather than by grace—and they fail miserably, because no one can keep the Law perfectly:

> For whoever keeps the whole law and yet stumbles in one point, he has become guilty of all (James 2:10).

Remember, the Holy Spirit can't move through us until He can get to us. If we resist His patient efforts, then we simply delay His blessings for us.

Being saved by grace means that "it is no longer *I* who live, but *Christ* lives in me" (Galatians 2:20, emphasis added). A belief system that continually says "I'm not worthy of God's anointing" is faulty and flesh focused. Because of Jesus, we *are* worthy. God sees us in light of the perfect redemptive act His Son performed on the cross; not in light of what our flesh did or didn't do, or can or cannot do.

> But God, being rich in mercy, because of His great love with which He loved us, even when we were dead in our transgressions, made us alive together with Christ (by grace you have been saved), and raised us up with Him, and seated us with Him in the heavenly places in Christ Jesus, so that in the ages to come He might show the surpassing riches of His grace in kindness toward us in Christ Jesus (Ephesians 2:4-6).

We need to begin to see ourselves the way our heavenly Father sees us: washed and cleansed from all unrighteousness (see 2 Peter 1:9).

WHAT SPIRIT-LED LOOKS LIKE

The Bible reveals a very interesting truth about the Spirit-led life: Spirit-led life is also Spirit dwelt. Isn't that amazing? The Spirit actually dwells *within us.*

In the Old Testament, the priest had to enter into the Holy of Holies in the Temple once a year to secure atonement for the people. Now, in the age following Christ's once-for-all act of atonement, *we* are the temple:

> Do you not know that you are a temple of God and that the Spirit of God dwells in you? (1 Corinthians 3:16).

God cares for and protects His temple. Verse 17 of 1 Corinthians 3 reads, "If any man destroys the temple of God, God will destroy him, for the temple of God is holy, and that is what you are." We need to remind the enemy that God will destroy anyone who tries to destroy the temple of God. We need to tell Satan, "Don't touch this temple! It was built by God!"

When Christ died on the cross, He bought sin and sickness. In that purchase, He saved us—He provided a way out of poverty, sickness and death. Because we are the temple of the Holy Spirit, God is as interested in saving our temple—our body—as He is our spirit.

We talked earlier about how the word "saved" is translated from the Greek *sozo*, which denotes the idea "to be made whole" (see chapter 1). God is interested in the *whole* of His temple. If we are the body of Christ and if we are His temple, then God wants not only to save the spirit of people but also to save His house. He wants to heal the Body of Christ. That's what salvation is—healing, restoring, putting us back into proper position so that God can accomplish on Earth what He intends to do through us.

Being the temple of God comes with a singular responsibility: to glorify Him with our body. First Corinthians 6:20 says, "For you have been bought with a price: therefore glorify God in your body." We are no longer our own. We belong to Christ and must be led by His Spirit, not by our own desires.

It's interesting how the Bible says to glorify God "*in your body.*" For those who say that the flesh is evil, this is proof that it is not. Once we've been born again, we are led by the Spirit—and this includes our body. Our body is not evil when the Spirit of God is guiding us. Instead, our body is freed and liberated to do God's work and to live the victorious Christian life.

THE ANOINTING OF THE HOLY SPIRIT

How do we accomplish God's will on Earth? Through the Holy Spirit's anointing in our life. Without the anointing, we just spend our time fighting and bickering rather than doing God's work.

When we come to Christ, we are commissioned to preach the gospel to all nations (see Mark 16:15; Luke 24:46-48; Acts 1:8). But God not only gives us His Word to preach; He also gives us His Spirit to equip us for the job.

In the Gospel of Mark, Jesus tells us that supernatural signs will follow the preaching of God's Word:

These signs will accompany those who have believed: in My name they will cast out demons, they will speak with new tongues; they will pick up serpents, and if they drink any deadly poison, it will not hurt them; they will lay hands on the sick, and they will recover (Mark 16:17-18).

God puts His Spirit in us to demonstrate His Word to the world. The lost walk by sight and need signs in order to believe. God has provided those signs. The purpose of anointing is not only for us to show people how good we are or how many wonderful things we do. The anointing is also for the world—for the lost, for the sick, for the hurting.

The anointing gives power to the believer to move into a life of overcoming all the obstacles brought against us in the world—obstacles either from our own flesh or from the enemy. When the Word of God comes to a believer, one of two things will happen: *revelation*, which leads to *action*; or *religion*, which results in *inaction*. God is clear in His Word as to which response He wants from us: *action*—we are to be doers of the Word:

> For if anyone is a hearer of the word and not a doer, he is like a man who looks at his natural face in a mirror; for once he has looked at himself and gone away, he has immediately forgotten what kind of person he was. *But* one who looks intently at the perfect law, the law of liberty, and abides by it, not having become a forgetful hearer but an effectual doer, this man will be blessed in what he does (James 1:23-25).

The anointing also gives us the knowledge that we need to fully serve God on the earth:

> But you have received the Holy Spirit and he lives within you, in your hearts, so that you don't need anyone to teach you what is right. For he teaches you all things, and he is the Truth, and no liar; and so, just as he has said, you must live in Christ, never to depart from him (1 John 2:27, *TLB*).

In other words, the Holy Spirit is our *Teacher*—but we have to abide in Him. If we don't abide in Him, we won't get the instruction and teaching we need to be His witness. We only have this anointing when we remain in the Holy Spirit.

How to Activate the Anointing

For many believers today, the Holy Spirit in them is like the Maytag repairman—you know, *never getting a chance to work!* This isn't how it should be. We need to have an accurate understanding of the Holy Spirit so that we can walk in His anointing and follow His leading in our life. This takes an activation of the anointing.

Before we can activate the anointing, however, we need to fully understand *what* the anointing is. The word "anointing" refers to a smearing or a rubbing. It is the endowment of the very characteristics, qualities and virtues of the Holy Spirit inside of us so that we are transformed from who we were to who He is.

If we're going to fully become the Body of Christ, then the Holy Spirit needs to be released to live in us so that He changes us from the inside out and so that the very character of God rubs off on us and begins to rise up within each of us. But this cannot happen until we submit ourselves to God totally so that we have our mind set on the Spirit and not on the flesh.

How to Celebrate Interdependence Day

In America, we are so independent minded that we even have a day of the year set aside to celebrate our independence. But God calls us to be *interdependent*, not independent. He wants us to be interdependent with the Holy Spirit—to know the Holy Spirit intimately, to have a relationship with the Holy Spirit so that He can fully work through us. It's about not wanting it "my way, right away." It's about submitting everything that we have to the Holy Spirit residing within us.

If we don't take this path, if we instead choose the *I can do it myself because I'm Mr. or Ms. Independent*-way, then we will be moving in pride—and pride inevitably leads to a fall. When we walk in pride, our mind focuses on the flesh, and that is a path that ends in devastation.

James 4:6 and 1 Peter 5:5 say, "God is opposed to the proud, but gives grace to the humble." When we humble ourselves under His mighty hand, He gives us grace. The anointing of the Holy Spirit then comes into us, and it's that anointing that begins to break the chains on our lives, giving us breakthroughs in those areas where we need to be set free.

How to Be Released in Power

Ephesians 3:20 says, "Now to Him who is able to do far more abundantly beyond all that we ask or think, according to the power that works within us." When we understand that there is an anointing by the Spirit of God in us, we have the ability to do and to achieve beyond what we could think of or ask for. God's power is at work within us. The word "power" is translated from the Greek word *dunamis,* which means "a wonderful force or miraculous strength." In other words, the anointing of the Holy Spirit in us releases God's power to get results in our lives—to win the battle.

Second Timothy 3:5 says, "Holding to a form of godliness, although they have denied its power; Avoid such men as these." The powerlessness described in this verse is the very opposite of Holy Spirit anointing. If we move by our own strength, by our own mind, then we're going to move just in form (not in truth), and we will be completely powerless. This happens when we become so entrenched in tradition that we are unwilling to change for the good of the Kingdom.

Yes, our God is unchanging, but His people should be *constantly* changing. Why? Because we are *in the process of being sanctified*, of being transformed more and more day by day into Christ's likeness. Without change, there is no growth. When we embrace the anointing, however, we are changed and we can grow.

You can't *think* big enough. You can't *ask* big enough. No matter how big you think or ask, you will receive beyond that, because it will come supernaturally. It will come through the anointing of the Holy Spirit as you submit yourself to Him and His leading in every situation.

How to Receive Anointing

So how do we receive this anointing—how is it activated in our lives? Isaiah said:

> Ho! Every one who thirsts, come to the waters; and you who have no money come, buy and eat. Come, buy wine and milk without money and without cost (Isaiah 55:1).

All people are invited and encouraged to come and drink, come and eat, free of charge! The anointing of the Holy Spirit can't be bought; it's free—but it comes with a cost. When we go to the grocery store, we give our money in order to receive a product. We make an exchange. It's the same in the spiritual realm. If we want the anointing, we have to make an exchange for it. The cost? Our *life*—every area of it. We give our time in prayer, our time in studying the Word, our time in fasting—and not just for a while but for our entire life.

Then, after we receive the anointing, we have to exercise it. It's like having barbells. Just owning the barbells won't make us stronger; it's what we do with them that determines our strength. In the same way, the anointing itself doesn't make us stronger; it's what we do with it that determines our strength.

If you've been resisting God's leading on your life, if you've been callous to the urging of the Holy Spirit, why not change today? Come to God in repentance for seeking after *your* ways instead of His. Be willing to release the things you've been hanging on to that have separated you from God. Cast them down and humble yourself before God. Cry out, "God, release Your Spirit inside of me."

> All of you, clothe yourselves with humility toward one another, because, "God opposes the proud but gives grace to the humble." Humble yourselves, therefore, under God's mighty hand, that he may lift you up in due time (1 Peter 5:5-6, *NIV*).

Notice that the passage above starts with "all of you." We're *all* supposed to do this, not just some of us. It's not an option. We are to collectively clothe ourselves with humility, to collectively get on our face before God and to collectively cry out so that God will release what He has for us.

God is very willing to release it. The problem is that *we* haven't been willing to receive it. We must come to a place where we humble ourselves, where we submit ourselves under God's hand and where we allow Him to exalt us at the proper time.

GOD'S FUEL FOR ANOINTING

In Spokane, there's a mansion that has been converted into a restaurant called Patsy Clark's. It's a very nice place with fairly high prices—$50 per head, on the low end. My wife and I had always wanted to eat there but never quite had the money. In the middle of a fast I was on, my wife did some calculating and discovered that this was the perfect opportunity to go—half the cost, since only one of us would be eating! Brilliant! So we went to Patsy Clark's, where my wife enjoyed this amazing dinner while I sipped a Diet Coke (next time she's fasting, that's where we're going!).

Fasting isn't easy. If you've ever done it, you know what I'm talking about. By about the third week, I was seeing hamburgers in the clouds!

Why does our body react in such peculiar ways when we're fasting? Why do we suddenly become so acutely aware, so sensitive, so in tune to this thing called *food*, which we normally take for granted? Because our bodies need it. There's a reason our stomach feels like it's going to eat itself when we start skipping meals: God made us to need food to stay alive. It's the fuel that keeps us going throughout the day, and if we go long enough without it, we won't be able to go anymore.

It's the same in the spiritual realm. We need a spiritual fuel to keep going. Without it, we get weak, and eventually we can't go any longer. Just as you can't thrive physically without food, you can't thrive spiritually without spiritual food.

What is our spiritual food? First and foremost, it's the Word of God. The Holy Spirit works through God's Word to grow spiritual fruit in our lives. This fruit is what *fuels* God's anointing in our lives.

> I will ask the Father, and He will give you another Helper, that He may be with you forever; that is the Spirit of truth, whom the world cannot receive, because it does not see Him or know Him, but you know Him because He abides with you and will be in you (John 14:16-17).

When Christ left this world, He sent the Holy Spirit in His place as "another Helper" to abide with us and to be in us. The purpose of the Helper was, first and foremost, to equip us to serve God by serving others.

Later in the same chapter of John, Jesus explained one of the functions of the Helper:

> But the Helper, the Holy Spirit, whom the Father will send in My name, He will teach you all things, and bring to your remembrance all that I said to you (John 14:26).

In other words, it is the Holy Spirit who helps us to recall Christ's teachings and to internalize them and live them out.

The Nine Gifts
The Bible lists nine gifts of "the manifestation of the Spirit," which are to be used "for the common good" of those around us

(1 Corinthians 12:7). God gives us these gifts so that we can serve others (see 1 Corinthians 12:8-10):

1. Word of wisdom
2. Word of knowledge
3. Gift of faith
4. Gifts of healings (the Greek is plural)
5. Working of miracles
6. Ability to prophesy
7. Discerning of spirits
8. Gift of tongues
9. Interpretation of tongues

All nine gifts are available to believers as the Spirit wills to release them, based on the needs of those being ministered to. Remember, it is the fruit that fuels us, feeding the gifts in our lives and allowing us to use the gifts for the good of others.

The Nine Fruits

There are also nine fruits of the Spirit (see Galatians 5:22-23):

1. Love
2. Joy
3. Peace
4. Patience
5. Kindness
6. Goodness
7. Faithfulness
8. Gentleness
9. Self-control

The fruits of the Spirit are God's image shining through us, the very character of God dwelling in us and being displayed for all to see.

> We have come to know and have believed the love which God has for us. God is love, and the one who abides in love abides in God, and God abides in him (1 John 4:16).

As the Scripture above reminds us, "God is love." When we love, we shine forth God's character to the world. It's the same with each of the other eight fruits. If God dwells in us by His Spirit and if the Spirit causes our character to become more and more like God's character, then, as the Spirit sanctifies us, we will begin to show more and more of these fruits in our lives. This, in turn, proves and displays our Christianity to the world, showing that we are conformed to Christ:

> For those whom He foreknew, He also predestined to become conformed to the image of His Son, so that He would be the firstborn among many brethren (Romans 8:29).

Becoming conformed to God's image isn't optional. As people of God, we have been *predestined* to be conformed to the image of God. We are Christ's Body and should exemplify all that the Head represents.

Counterfeit Fruits

The very end of verse 23 in Galatians 5 reads, "Against such things there is no law." In other words, no law of man can be orchestrated against God in us. The power of the Spirit's fruits is so strong that no mere law can be set against it and nothing can stop it. However, that's not to say that people (or powers) won't *try* to stop it. In fact, Satan is very busy producing what I call *counterfeit fruits* in people's lives: instead of love, they have hate. In place of joy, they have depression. They don't have peace; instead, they have anxiety, unrest and worry. Fear replaces faith. Impatience crowds out patience. And so on.

Unfortunately, too many people in the Body of Christ have gotten caught up in counterfeit fruits. The problem is that these fruits won't fuel a life whose chief focus is serving God.

Many of the people we pray for in the Healing Rooms have allowed their mind to focus on the flesh rather than on the Spirit. They've become enmeshed in these counterfeit fruits, and most of the time they don't even realize it. When we embody the counterfeit, the gift of the Spirit becomes corrupted. How can we have the fruit of healing when we are filled with hate, envy, fear or greed?

What's the solution? *Breaking the bonds of the counterfeit and replacing it with the real thing.* For those caught in depression, for example, we banish that depression and call forth the joy of the Lord. Or when people are consumed by hate or bitterness, through the Holy Spirit they can be brought to a point of forgiveness and love. When the counterfeit flees, a void where the real thing—the Holy Spirit's fruits—can come and dwell is left behind. Only then can God's people be empowered to live and walk in the Spirit's ways.

Progressive Fruits

We know that God listed the fruits of the Holy Spirit in the order that they are in for a purpose. Love is first. Why? Because you can't have the next fruit (joy) without having love first. And you can't have peace (the third fruit) until you have joy. It's progressive.

Love is foundational because it's the greatest commandment:

> And He said to him, "You shall love the Lord your God with all your heart, and with all your soul, and with all your mind." This is the great and foremost commandment. The second is like it, "You shall love your neighbor as yourself" (Matthew 22:37-39).

Many other verses also speak on the primacy of love:

> There is no fear in love; but perfect love casts out fear, because fear involves punishment, and the one who fears is not perfected in love (1 John 4:18).

> But now faith, hope, love, abide these three; but the greatest of these is love (1 Corinthians 13:13).

> You did not choose Me but I chose you, and appointed you that you would go and bear fruit, and that your fruit should remain, so that whatever you ask of the Father in My name He may give to you. This I command you, that you love one another (John 15:16-17).

If I speak with the tongues of men and of angels, but do not have love, I have become a noisy gong or a clanging cymbal. And if I have the gift of prophecy, and know all mysteries and all knowledge; and if I have all faith, so as to remove mountains, but do not have love, I am nothing. And if I give all my possessions to feed the poor, and if I surrender my body to be burned, but do not have love, it profits me nothing (1 Corinthians 13:1-3).

God is very clear: As we are empowered by the Spirit to serve Him by serving others, *love* must be at the center of it all.

THE AUTHORITY OF THE HOLY SPIRIT

Whenever we are busy for God, there will always be someone busy trying to stop us: Satan. The enemy does not want to see us advancing God's kingdom or bringing healing, and he will do all he can to stop it. He will try very hard, but *try* is really all he can do. Remember, the end of the story has already been written—and the devil doesn't win. God wins. And we, as God's people, get to take part in that victory.

As we've learned, the authority we as believers have been given is authority over *all* the power of our enemy (see Luke 10:19). We don't have *some* authority; we have *all* authority. The word "power" is translated from the Greek word *exousia*, which means "delegated influence: authority, jurisdiction, liberty, power, right, strength." In other words, King Jesus has delegated His influence to us so that we have authority over Satan.

Truly I say to you, whatever you shall bind on earth shall have been bound in heaven; and whatever you loose on earth shall have been loosed in heaven (Matthew 18:18).

Authority gives us the power to bind and loose on Earth. We become the authority of God on the earth. We can pray with authority, and we can walk in authority. We move with such authority in the Spirit that the enemy can't even touch us. We've got the whole armor of God covering us, and no matter how many fiery darts Satan sends our way, they're extinguished before we even feel the heat.

We can stand firm against the enemy, because we know where our strength comes from:

Finally, be strong in the Lord and in the strength of His might. Put on the full armor of God, so that you will be able to stand firm against the schemes of the devil (Ephesians 6:10-11).

God's power is greater than Satan's, and when it's God's power working in us through the Holy Spirit, we no longer need to be fearful or trembling. We can conquer in confidence.

You are from God, little children, and have overcome them; because greater is He who is in you than he who is in the world (1 John 4:4).

Resist the devil and he will flee from you (James 4:7).

We can't wrap our mind around the reality of our authority, however, until our mind has been renewed. But once it has been renewed, the truth of our spiritual power (which is woven throughout Scripture) becomes undeniably clear: we're able to be strong, stand firm and realize just how much power and might we have in the Lord!

> Be strong in the Lord and in the power of His might
> (Ephesians 6:10, *NKJV*).

The Bible tells us that all authority was given to Christ: "Jesus came up and spoke to them, saying, 'All authority has been given to Me in heaven and on earth'" (Matthew 28:18). Later, in the book of Ephesians, we learn that this authority of Christ's was transferred to *us*, as His Body. We have the very power of the resurrection that raised Jesus from the dead available to us through the Holy Spirit living in us:

> I pray that the eyes of your heart may be enlightened, so that you will know what is the hope of His calling, what are the riches of the glory of His inheritance in the saints, and *what is the surpassing greatness of His power toward us who believe.* These are in accordance with the working of the strength of His might which He brought about in Christ, when He raised Him from the dead and seated Him at His right hand in the heavenly places, far above all rule and authority and power and dominion, and every name that is named, not only in this age but also in the one to come. And He put all things in subjection

under His feet, and gave Him as head over all things to the church, which is His body, the fullness of Him who fills all in all (Ephesians 1:18-23, emphasis added).

Note the phrase "the surpassing greatness of His power toward us who believe" (v. 19), which refers to the Holy Spirit in us. Since we are the Body of Christ (and therefore God's vessels for showing Christ's love and healing on Earth), power has been entrusted to us—the very power that was Christ's power during His days on Earth.

The Ephesians 1 passage goes on to say, "He put all things in subjection under His feet, and gave Him as head over all things to the church, which is His body, the fullness of Him who fills *all in all*" (vv. 22-23, emphasis added). Note that the last verse doesn't read "the fullness of Him who fills *some in some*." The word "all" means *all!* That's the dominion and the power that God gave us when He raised Christ from the dead and when we were raised with Him. We were seated with Him in heavenly places because we are to be His Body. This isn't something that is *going* to happen in the future. This is something that has *already* happened. The same Holy Spirit who raised Jesus has already raised us up with Him so that we can be His Body. The authority that the Father gave to Jesus is available to us *now*.

We have an enemy to conquer, but we can't overcome him unless we walk in the authority to do so.

What Authority Looks Like

I have a vision of how authority works for believers. If I went down to an intersection with a traffic light and tried to direct traffic, dressed in nothing more than jeans and a T-shirt, what would happen? People would obviously not be very happy. I might even get run over! But if I were hired by the police department and had a police uniform on, I could walk into that intersection, hold up my hand and direct traffic with no problem. People would obey me. Why? Because now they could recognize my authority. My uniform would indicate the authority that sent me: the police department.

That's the way it works for Christians, too. As believers, we are sent by God's authority. Therefore, we have all the authority that He has given to us. If we tried defeating the enemy without our cloak of authority—without our spiritual armor—we'd be in trouble. But once we're robed in Christ and equipped with our spiritual armor, we can walk in all authority and carry out our God-given assignment, spreading God's gospel and preaching His ultimate healing here on Earth:

> Our gospel did not come to you in word only, but also in power and in the Holy Spirit and with full conviction (1 Thessalonians 1:5).

Why We Can Pray and Live in Authority

In closing, here's a list of Bible verses to stand on in claiming and using our healing authority under God. Copy this list and post it where you'll see it often. It is a wonderful reminder that because of the Holy Spirit, you can walk in authority and be victorious in your life:

- Isaiah 54:17—Because no weapon formed against you can prosper

- Mark 11:23—Because you can move mountains
- Luke 10:19—Because you have authority over all the power of your enemy
- John 14:12—Because you will do works greater than those of Christ
- Romans 8:37—Because you are more than a conqueror
- Romans 16:20—Because your enemy is beneath your feet
- 1 Corinthians 15:57—Because you are a victor and not a victim
- 2 Corinthians 5:21—Because you are the righteousness of Christ
- Ephesians 6:16—Because you are able to extinguish all the fiery darts from the enemy
- Philippians 4:19—Because your God shall supply everything you need
- Colossians 2:10—Because you are the head and not the tail
- Hebrews 4:16—Because you can come boldly before the throne of God
- 1 John 2:27—Because you have an anointing and you know all things
- 1 John 4:4—Because the One who is in you is greater than the enemy

We've been given authority by God Himself. And as we come under His subjection and make ourselves interdependent with Him, we have all the authority of heaven and Earth for the fulfillment of His will to flow into this realm.

Praise God, we have His authority to heal! Let's use it.

6

FAITH FOR
Healing

THE CREATIVE POWER OF FAITH

God's will is a creative force because it is the will of the Initiator, the Creator, and will not be fruitless—because *He* is its source. *Knowing* that fact is what releases His creative force within us too. That knowing, that believing, that *faith* in God's inerrant Word, is what then moves the will of God into its creative form so that we can receive His promises and perform His will in dealing with the needs of people around us. It is His Word that produces the faith in us in the first place—which is what then moves His will into its creative form.

> So will My word be which goes forth from My mouth;
> it will not return to Me empty, without accomplishing
> what I desire, and without succeeding in the matter for
> which I sent it (Isaiah 55:11).

The power of God's Word benefits us in direct proportion to our faith in His Word (see Matthew 9:29). Thus, faith in the

Word of God brings about fulfillment for us and pleases God (remember, without faith it's impossible to please God—see Hebrews 11:6).

In John 15:7, we are told that if we abide in God and His Word abides in us, then we can ask whatever we wish, and it will be done for us. The key here is that we *abide* in God, press in to Him, dwell in His ways, continue in His light.

In Romans 4:16, Paul says that Abraham is the father of our faith. When we read through Genesis 12–25, it becomes clear that Abraham's faith-walk was characterized by listening to and depending on God's voice, embracing the words and promises God gave him, and then stepping out to obey God's word to him—even in cases when the consequences were risky, intimidating and painful. In the same way, walking in faith means that we listen to what the Holy Spirit is saying to us, embrace God's Word, let it abide in us, and walk in obedience to it, so that we can see the creative power of God released in our lives.

House of Faith

Faith can be compared to building a house: The building materials are not the house; they are the substance the house is made of. It's what we do with the substance that determines whether or not we will have a house. If we don't believe that the substance can produce a house, then we won't act on it, the substance (the building materials) will sit there unproductive, and a house will never be seen. But when we move from seeing the materials to doing something with them, we begin to create a house.

God has a plan for us. He wants to involve us in building His house, the Church! His material is the Word of God, which produces faith. He will not build the house all on His own. He wants to partner in relationship with us to build it.

When we choose by our own free will to obey God's will and when we begin to create and establish His kingdom on Earth, we build God's house.

I pose to you the same question Jesus asked in Acts 7:49: What kind of house are you building for God?

Necessity of Faith

So often people have a wrong perspective on faith. I even hear people say things such as, "I don't want to get my hopes too high." These people are trying to move in healing, but they're afraid to do so by faith because they don't want their hopes dashed in case nothing happens—they're setting themselves up for failure by inviting doubt to take over. But faith is necessary in the believer so that we can experience the will of God in our lives.

Part of the key is in understanding the word "hope." Hebrews 11:1 tells us that "faith is the assurance of things hoped for" and the evidence "of things not seen." The word "hoped" in that verse means trust. In other words, when people say, "I don't want to get my hopes too high," what they are really saying is, "I don't want to have too much trust, or faith, in God's power, because if I do, I might be disappointed. I might look for my healing but not receive it." It's as if they're almost giving God some wiggle room for failure so that they can then say, "Well, I prayed—and I'm sure He did His best, but it just didn't happen."

That thinking is in direct conflict with God's Word:

Without faith it is impossible to please Him, for he who comes to God must believe that He is and that He is a rewarder of those who seek Him (Hebrews 11:6).

Our level of hope must be determined by the level of our expectation. If we hope for much, then we are to have much faith—we maintain a high level of assurance that we will receive what we hope for. If we don't have hope, then we might as well not even worry about faith, because faith is the assurance, the expectant drive, that will deliver what we are hoping for. Using an automobile analogy, if gasoline is the Holy Spirit and faith is the engine, then hope is the key. Lack of hope, therefore, is like having the car all gassed up and ready to go . . . and not even looking for the key.

The only reason people wouldn't want to get their hopes too high is that sometimes people measure by their past failures the things they desire. Hope must be the target of faith to bring God's promise into believers. Hope is the future—something promised and yet to come. It's like that house. We must have a hope that literally *sees* the house built in our mind's eye and *knows* that it's what we *do* with the materials (the substance of faith) that will bring the house to reality.

Activation of Faith

Faith is activated in the unseen realm from the time we ask according to the will of God until we see the end result in the natural. When we can see it in the natural, faith stops, because it has had its effect on that hope and prayer and now moves on to the next hope and prayer.

Faith is only for the unseen realm that lies ahead, as the apostle Paul said:

Forgetting what lies behind and reaching forward to what lies ahead, I press on toward the goal for the prize of the upward call of God in Christ Jesus (Philippians 3:13-14).

It's the same with healing. Our hope (for the healing we want manifested) is evidenced by exercising our faith in God's Word of truth. The goal of faith is future reality. But if we hope we're healed and we don't *know* we're healed by faith, then we cannot confess those things that are not as though they were (see Romans 4:17).

So faith, in believers, is a reality of what we hope for. We just *know* it. And we know it because the Word of God is truth; and that truth is evidence in the realm of the spirit, waiting to be revealed in the natural realm. And it's all based on what we *do*.

Our hope needs to be anchored in the will of God, because His will is a reality greater than anything it could produce in the natural. Faith in God has no limits—neither in the natural realm nor in the supernatural sphere.

When hope, will and faith come together, God's promise is fulfilled in the believer.

Lining Up Our Faith

"Hope deferred makes the heart sick, but desire fulfilled is a tree of life" (Proverbs 13:12). The word "sick" means to be ill or receptive to sickness. Sometimes people say, "I hope I'm healed."

But when we say that, we create a receptivity to the sickness, because when we imply that we know we're not healed, we are acknowledging that we are actually *not* healed (but are only *hoping* we are); and we are, in effect, confessing that we're sick. But remember, faith requires us to *confess what is not as though it were* so that the will of God can come into us.

Instead of hoping we're healed, we each need to confess, "I *am* healed!" Rather than our confession lining up with what the devil does to make us sick, our confession needs to line up with the creating will of God, which makes us well because it's a greater force than anything the enemy could ever throw at us.

THE RELATIONAL VEHICLE OF GOD

Our faith is the relational vehicle that God uses to fulfill the physical manifestation of His Word through us. It keeps us connected to Him. In that connection, our will is lined up with His so that by faith His will can be done through us.

To the natural person, faith is a risky business, because it takes us where we can't see—and the natural person wants to walk by sight. To the natural person, healing by faith seems ridiculous. But we must do what appears ridiculous so that God can do what is miraculous (see 1 Corinthians 1:27).

When we walk by faith, obviously we don't see our healing in the beginning, because it doesn't exist yet *here in the natural realm*; our faith is in the process of bringing it forth through the power of the Holy Spirit.

Everything seen was at one time unseen. Thus, all natural things come from the supernatural realm. It is what we do with the supernatural that determines its impact in the natural. "God is Spirit" (John 4:24), He has a kingdom (a supernatural realm), and He has a creating will for us within that realm. His Word, living and active, is what produces faith in us, which also becomes living and active. In this way, God's will can be done on Earth—through our living and active faith bringing what is in the supernatural realm of God into our natural realm.

Here is an example of how this works: A mother is cooking dinner and has a vision of a chocolate cake with chocolate frosting for dessert. What does Mom do? She puts all of the substance of the cake out on the kitchen table: the flour, water, sugar, baking soda, cocoa and baking chocolate—all of the ingredients that make the cake. Notice that she doesn't put all of the substance of the cake out on the kitchen table and then get down on her knees, look up toward heaven and pray, "Oh great and heavenly God, I beg You now, bring forth *cake!*" No! She mixes the substance together, she turns on the heat, she puts it in the oven, and her substance soon becomes reality. Cake!

Whether or not she will see the cake isn't determined by what God does; it's determined by *what she does with the substance.* Even when the children come into the house before dessert has been started and they ask, "Hey, Mom, what's for dessert?" she confesses things that are not as though they were when she smiles and tells them, "We're having chocolate cake."

So what is more real, the substance or the cake? If you don't believe that the substance is more real than the cake, then just try to get that cake made without the substance—the ingredients. Try to put all of the elements out on the countertop and go into your deepest prayer ever that God will take them all and whip you up a nice cake. It won't happen!

Faith is the substance of things hoped for and the evidence of something not yet seen. Our confidence is rewarded when Mom puts the substance out there and becomes a *doer* of bringing about the resulting cake—all because she had a vision of that cake. It's in what she *does* that causes that substance to begin to take shape and become a reality greater than what it originally was. It's what we do about what we don't yet see that determines what we will soon see.

We must come to a place where we no longer doubt our faith, but we doubt our doubt; because faith is set on the will of God, and doubt is set on nothing. Faith establishes it. Doubt leaves it out. Faith rests on far more solid ground than the evidence of our senses.

Two Faiths

There are two kinds of faith: *produced* faith and *prevailing* faith. *Produced faith* comes to us when we get into the Word of God. *Prevailing faith* is produced faith acted upon as we become doers of the Word. Prevailing faith overcomes the supernatural realm so that it can come into the natural realm.

First John 5:4 says, "Whatever is born of God overcomes the world [the natural realm]; and this is the victory that has overcome the world—our faith." Faith is an irresistible force. It can overcome the world. It can overcome every obstacle. It has no limits. Faith is the *pre*incarnate existence of what you do not yet have.

People struggle with faith far too often. It's as though they're looking for something but don't want to make the effort to go get it. True faith in believers will not focus on denying that we're sick; it will simply establish that we are healed. Our healing cannot even begin until we know that we're healed more than we know we're sick.

Some people say things like, "I don't want to walk by faith because if I go to the doctor and I'm confessing those things that aren't as though they are, and I'm telling the doctor, 'I'm healed' and he examines me and decides that I'm not coming from his perspective, then he'll say to me, 'You're in denial!'"

We need to look at the doctor and say, "Doc, you're absolutely right. I am in denial. I deny everything the devil is trying to do to me!"

Let's start denying the devil and stop denying God.

Fearless Faith

Fearlessness is the occupation of faith. When we're faithful, we're fearless. Faith is the Word in progress. Faith changes our future.

Sight causes us to confess against faith. Faith takes over sight and confesses the healing so that it will appear. Vision becomes reality when we walk by faith—it's the vision of the cake Mom is fixing for dessert. Faith moves the vision into its creative form. When we confess those things that are not, when we speak to what isn't, when we speak God's will, what *isn't* rushes into *being*, and our own voice becomes the audible sound of God's will taking place on the earth.

The key to getting the sick healed isn't in what we possess; it's in God who possesses us—He causes us to move by faith. Too many people are in failure because they're not moving in faith. When we move by sight, it's so easy for the enemy to bind us up. He does his best work in the realm of sight and prefers that we not walk in the "pre-sight" realm of faith.

Expectant Faith

We have to believe that we already have from God what we pray for *at the time we pray and ask*. Jesus confirms this plainly in Mark 11:24, where He tells us that whatever we ask for in prayer, when we believe that we have what we asked for, what we asked for will be ours.

All answered prayer comes when we meet the one and only condition God asks of us: *expectant faith*.

> It shall be done to you according to your faith (Matthew 9:29).

We receive from God by the measure of our faith. And the measure of our faith is determined by the measure of the Word we get within us and then walk in.

So what's the maximum receiving for the maximum faith? *All things*:

> All things are possible to him who believes (Mark 9:23).

Mark 9:23 is a powerful Scripture. It says very clearly that if we believe that God is a rewarder of His children and that His will has already been given to us fulfilled, then when we believe unquestioningly in Him, nothing shall be impossible for us. In other words, there are *no limits* in our life! We can do all things through Christ who is our strength, and we can move in an unlimited capacity because we're in alignment with God.

First John 5:14 says, "This is the confidence we have in approaching God: that if we ask anything according to his will, he hears us" (*NIV*). The will of God produces faith. We can have a high confidence in God because we ask according to His will. The passage goes on to say, "And if we know that he hears us—whatever we ask—we know that we have what we asked of him" (1 John 5:15, *NIV*). It doesn't say we *might* get it; it says that we *have it.*

The key is what *we* do with the Word, not what God does with the Word. God doesn't need to fulfill His will. *We* fulfill it— by being doers of His Word. Ephesians 3:20 says that this comes "according to the power that works within us." When we have a relationship with the Holy Spirit, the power of the Holy Spirit in us releases God's creating will.

So the answer to all prayer is in His will being fulfilled through us as we believe that we have received at the time we pray and ask. And that believing is then expressed as we confess those things that are not as though they are.

Romans 3:3 poses the question, "What if some did not have faith? Will their lack of faith nullify God's faithfulness?" (*NIV*). The answer comes in the next verse: "Not at all!" (v. 4). The fact that we're praying for somebody when there are people around us who don't believe doesn't change the faithfulness of God. *Our* belief is what God is looking for.

Asset-Filled Faith

Faith takes God's will and, by the authority He vests in us, makes His will our own. Faith is such a powerful force that it can set us into wholeness (see Mark 5:34). Faith is an incredible asset within every believer, as the following verses tell us:

- Luke 18:42—"Your faith has healed you."
- Acts 15:9—We're purified by faith.
- Acts 26:18—We're "sanctified by faith."
- Romans 3:28—We're "justified by faith."
- Romans 3:30—We're spiritually "circumcised by faith."
- Romans 3:31—We're moved by faith to "uphold the law."
- Romans 4:13—The promises of God are granted through faith.
- Romans 12:6—Spiritual gifts are released in proportion to our faith.
- Hebrews 10:38—The just "will live by faith."
- Hebrews 11:1—Faith is the substance of things hoped for.
- Hebrews 11:6—"Without faith it is impossible to please God."
- Hebrews 11:33—Faith allows us to subdue kingdoms.
- Hebrews 11:39—Good reports come by faith.
- Hebrews 12:2—God is the author and finisher of our faith.
- James 1:6—Faith overcomes doubt.
- 1 John 5:4—Faith allows us to overcome the world.

We should take each of these verses and get into our spirit how crucial, unstoppable and powerful faith is!

THE ENEMY OF FAITH

Our faith is on trial by the work of the devil, who wants nothing more than to steal the Word from us and show us all kinds of devastation in our lives. He shows us our past failures. He points to negative circumstances. He accuses us of being worthless, sick, weak—failures. He does all he can to cause us to twist our belief system so that we believe what we see in the enemy's portrayal of things. His goal is to get our confession of being limited by our circumstances—"Well, I guess under the circumstances, I can't do it."

What we face is what we embrace. We need to learn to no longer face our enemy but turn our back on him and face our God. If we make God the full-time God over all areas of our life, then the devil will move on to easier targets. We turn our back on the enemy: We have authority and power over him!

I've seen cases where people have been so problem-centered that they've prevented themselves from being Christ-centered. When we're problem-centered, our focus is on everything about us, rather than all about Him. And while we know that there is a God of deliverance in one place, we're off over there in some other place. We're wallowing in all of our "problemness"—our negative circumstances—and crying out, "Oh God, come and deliver me!" But just maybe, God might be saying, "I'm not coming into that mess you've created! If you want to get delivered, maybe you need to leave the influence of the enemy, come to where I am and get out of all that junk." Deliverance requires us to move out of where we are and into where God is.

Growth and the Flow of Fearless Faith

To understand the relationship between faith and healing, we have to realize that we essentially get what we expect. The flow of a fearless, healing faith works like this:

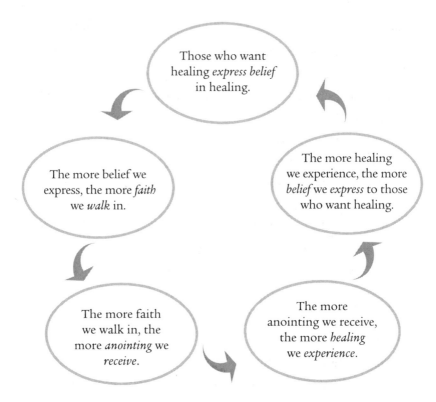

That is the perpetually creative power of faith.

Faith is about *growth*. We have to grow in God and move out of our problem centeredness. We can't walk in faith when we're living in fear. We can't walk on water while we're sitting in the boat. In order to walk on the water, we have to get out of the boat, walk by faith and keep our eyes on Jesus. Then it won't matter how deep the water is, because He will hold us up. We're no longer subject to the natural realm. We're no longer captive to what the enemy is doing in our life. And when the enemy finally figures out he can't move us, he'll stop wasting his time with us.

When we're moved only by God, listening to and obeying His voice and His Word alone, then we live and move in Him and are free from what the enemy wants to bring against us. We are faith-filled. We become fearless. Then we begin to walk in the power God created us to dwell in!

7

DIVINE *Health*

ESTABLISHED BY GOD'S WILL

It is important that we understand God's ultimate goal for the Body of Christ: It is *not* that the Body of Jesus be afflicted with sickness (which comes from the enemy). It *is* that we would wear the armor that comes from God that would extinguish all the fiery darts of sickness and that would establish divine health in us.

When we are healed from a sickness, we don't receive that healing in order to get sick all over again. Nowhere in the first chapter of the Bible does it say, "Let there be sickness." God created humanity without sickness. Sickness came through the Fall of humanity. As we learned in Galatians 3:13, we have been redeemed from the curse, which includes sickness. So why live under the curse that we have been redeemed from?

Healing is the process of establishing divine health in the Body of Jesus. In fact, He came that we might be healed and not have any sickness in us.

> Do you not know that your bodies are members of Christ? (1 Corinthians 6:15).

If our bodies are members of Christ and He's the Head, then should there be sickness in His Body? Of course not. As the apostle Paul said:

For those whom He foreknew, He also predestined to become conformed to *the image of His Son,* so that He would be the firstborn among many brethren (Romans 8:29, emphasis added).

What is the image of God's Son supposed to look like? Is the Body of Jesus to exemplify all that the Head represents? Of course. Paul says in 1 Corinthians 2:16 that "we have the mind of Christ." We have the mind of Christ because we're the Body of Christ. If we have the mind of Christ, then there should not be so many insecure people in the Body of Christ. We need to have the secure mind of Christ, which gives us the revelation of the fact that it's God's desire that we be well.

The enemy who comes against us wants us to have an earthly perspective that measures God by the condition of a Body of Christ that is sick rather than to have a truth that sets us free from sickness. First Corinthians 3:16-17 states, "Do you not know that you are a temple of God and that the Spirit of God dwells in you? If any man destroys the temple of God, God will destroy him, for the temple of God is holy, and that is what you are." As Christians, we are holy temples where God's Holy Spirit resides. If anyone touches the temple or attempts to destroy it, God will destroy the attacker. We ought to tell that to the devil. "Don't touch me, devil! I'm a holy temple of God!" We have that very authority in Christ, who gives us the power to move in divine health. We merely have to *know* it.

When was the last time you prayed for somebody to have divine health after the person was healed? You can't wrap your mind around something that your mind has not been renewed to. We need to renew our mind to the fact that divine health is God's will for us. If our mind is not renewed, we will conform to the world's order of things rather than to God's order, and we will pull the Word of God down to the level of our circumstances rather than raising our circumstances up to the level of the Word.

The Greatest Measure

"For you were bought with a price, therefore glorify God in your body and in your spirit, which are God's" (1 Corinthians 6:20, *NKJV*). Apostle Paul calls on us to glorify God in our body and in our spirit. We can glorify God in the midst of any trial we go through. But we don't glorify God because the devil has made us sick. We glorify God based on what Jesus has done to establish healing, which then establishes divine health.

Jesus tells us emphatically in John 14:13-14, "Whatever you ask in My name, that will I do, so that the Father may be glorified in the Son. If you ask Me anything in My name, I will do it." "The Father may be glorified in the Son" means that God gets the glory when we get the benefit of what the Son has done to heal us. The measure of the glory is determined by the measure of the benefit. So the greatest measure of glory that can go to the Father happens when there is nothing of the devil in us—no sin, no sickness.

Too many believers don't believe this is an attainable state for us to walk in. Yet that is exactly what the Word says we can walk in:

> Therefore you are to be perfect, as your heavenly Father is perfect (Matthew 5:48).

Those are the words of Jesus Himself. Would Jesus tell us to do something that was impossible for us to do? Sin is a choice. Therefore, we can choose not to sin. Many Christians don't believe this is possible, so they never attempt it and, therefore, never achieve it. But Romans 8:13 says that we *can* put the sins of our flesh to death by the power of the Holy Spirit!

More than anything else, doubt is the greatest destroyer of our potential. The works of the devil may not prevent as much achievement as our own doubt does. I sometimes wonder how many incredible things people haven't even attempted to accomplish in the Lord, all because they doubted either His power or their authority.

A Whole New Understanding

Our past concepts of God come from a *fallen-nature* understanding, rather than a *"restorational"* understanding. If we've been redeemed from the curse, then our redemptive state means that we are no longer subject to the curse from which we've been redeemed.

> My son, give attention to my words; incline your ear to my sayings. Do not let them depart from your sight;

keep them in the midst of your heart. For they are life to those who find them and health to all their body (Proverbs 4:20-22).

It's not a case where part of God is impacting only part of us so that we have some healing now and then and we're sick once in a while. The word "health" means a wholeness—to *all* our flesh, not just some of it. Our God is *Jehovah Rapha*, the God of wholeness. When He uses the word "health," He means *good* health.

Now may the God of peace Himself sanctify you entirely; and may your spirit and soul and body be preserved complete, without blame at the coming of our Lord Jesus Christ (1 Thessalonians 5:23).

This sanctification (or wholeness) message needs to be understood and accepted by all believers.

It is interesting how that message came to me. I was doing something at home and the Holy Spirit spoke to me. The Holy Spirit has a way of getting our attention. Most of the time, for me, it's when I'm mowing the lawn, doing some yard work or washing the car. On this particular occasion, I was puttering with something and the Holy Spirit suddenly asked me, "Do you know that healing was never meant to be for My Body?"

A statement like that will get your attention. I asked, "What do you mean, healing was not for Your Body?"

He replied, "Healing was not supposed to be for My Body, because My Body was not supposed to be sick in the first place."

Talk about revelation! Of course His Body wasn't supposed to be sick! Sometimes for us humans, the simplest concepts elude us until one day we're struck with one of those "Aha!" moments, and an idea we should have grasped long ago suddenly hits us.

"Healing," the Holy Spirit continued, "was supposed to be a sign to the lost of who I am. Divine health is for My Body, which has nothing of the enemy in it—not sin, not sickness." He added, "If you only teach on healing, it will keep you where you are, dealing with sickness. But if you bring the message of *divine health*, it will deliver you out of sickness and into the miraculous." Amazing.

Our God is an unchangeable God, but the condition of the Body of Jesus must be in *constant change*. It's called *growth*. We must constantly be moved to the highest levels of revelation. When we stop growing, we lose ground and the enemy overcomes us. Therefore, to move in divine healing is to walk in a dominion that we've been redeemed into. Healing is in the outer court. Divine health is in the inner court. Divine health is when we are truly connected with Jesus—where we live and move and have our being in Him. It is when we're connected to the Head with such power that all God has is exhibited in us and through us—then the enemy can't move us any longer. He can't bring what he has against us, because we no longer receive it—we no longer even acknowledge it.

A Constant Dominion

To walk in dominion we must be restored to it. We can't have restoration unless we have a reversal. Revelation brings a reversal because it moves us in another direction. When revelation of the truth comes that divine health is the optimum "children's bread," a reversal will happen as a matter of course, and we will come out of sickness and enter the realm of divine health.

The Body of Christ must be redirected from being merely healed to moving into the realm of divine health. Then the Father receives the optimum glory of the benefit of what Jesus did for us. Our salvation restores us back to how God created us to be in the beginning: creatures of divine health.

Second Corinthians 5:17 says, "If anyone is in Christ, he is a new creation; old things have passed away; behold, all things have become new" (*NJKV*). The term "new creation" means original formation. This means that we go back—as in before sin and sickness—into the original formation God created us to be in.

If we live in the Creator, then we can move in creative power. When the prophet Micah said, "Even the former dominion will come" (Micah 4:8), he was prophesizing about the former dominion that would come when Christ redeemed us from the curse of the Fall. In that redemptive state, we can take our former position—as it was prior to the Fall—the position that had no sickness in it: the divine health position.

Acts 17:28 says, "In Him we live and move and have our being." If there's no sickness in God and we are to live in Him, then we live in a place where no sickness can overcome us. We cannot have dominion over creation in this realm without the Creator releasing us into it. The Father released the Son into dominion, as evidenced by Jesus' words in Matthew 28:18: "All authority has been given to Me in heaven and on earth." There's the dominion, the authority. The Son released us into it as the

Body of Christ, where we have power "over all the power of the enemy" (Luke 10:19). There's a fullness of God when we have on His armor. When we live in Him, we have what He has.

We can't step into God and His armor and not get what He has. When we are in God, we get the fullness that He has made available to us. His fullness has divine health in it. His fullness is available to *all* the Body of Christ, not just some of it. Ephesians 6:16 talks about the armor of God quenching all the fiery darts of the enemy. We cannot have divine health unless we know the authority we have. Dominion is achieved when there is nothing of the enemy in us and we are only moving in God. Dominion is achieved when the supernatural becomes natural to us. When we know this, we can move in the greater reality of the kingdom of God.

Dominion releases the Kingdom, and the Kingdom establishes the divine. If the Kingdom is within us, if we have the Holy Spirit residing inside of us, that is more than sufficient power to establish divine health.

If I cast out demons by the Spirit of God, then the kingdom of God has come upon you (Matthew 12:28).

The kingdom of God is not something that comes and goes. It resides in believers constantly. It is a power seat of God in believers (see Luke 17:21). It is our authority backed up with His power. It's the kingdom, the reign, the dominion of God, to establish divine health. Therefore, we have a constant flow of creative power residing in us with which we can establish divine health—all by the *resurrection power* of the Holy Spirit.

Supernatural Healing

First Corinthians 2:14 tells us that the flesh of humanity cannot understand the things of God. Thus, we cannot understand divine health from a natural position. Our mind can't wrap around the concept of supernatural healing. When God is in the house, the house of God begins to move in what God wants in that house—and sickness isn't part of what He wants.

God *is* divine health, because there is no sickness in Him. So if the Spirit of God is dwelling in us and there is no sickness in the Holy Spirit, then that authority and power (which establishes divine health) is available to us. But our mind must be renewed to it, because the establishment of it depends on what we do to line up with God's will, to transform us from who we are into who He is.

When we live the Word, we operate above the law of sin and death. Divine health is the will of God so that the Body of Jesus would begin to look like Jesus. If we are the Body of Jesus, we should look like Him. If there is no sickness in Him, there should be none in us. He bore it on the cross so that we wouldn't have to in the world.

He was raised in a place of victory, and we were raised with Him. We need to begin to look like the Body of Christ and have nothing of the enemy in us. Our authority is to have power over *all* the power of the enemy.

We *can* walk in divine health! As our mind is renewed and we are no longer conformed to the natural realm of the world's way of thinking, we will no longer think it's normal to be sick—not even occasionally.

CREATED TO BE WELL

In the Garden there was no sickness. In heaven there is no sickness. Do you recall a passage of Scripture that told about when Jesus was sick and had to rest up and recover? *No!* That never once happened in His life.

Paul told the Colossians, "For in Christ there is all of God in a human body" (Colossians 2:9, *TLB*). This verse confirms that all the fullness of the provision of heaven is available to us. How? Because *we* are the Body of Christ. The passage goes on to say, "In Him you have been made complete" (Colossians 2:10). The word "complete" in this verse means *to make replete* or *to abundantly supply*. God is saying, "I have abundantly supplied." If we are so filled with the Lord, there will be no space for the devil to occupy. If we have been made complete, then we should not live incomplete. We have the wholeness of God in us. We're a new creation, recreated in the image of Jesus, predestined to be conformed to His image.

> Since you died with Christ to the basic principles of this world, why, as though you still belonged to it, do you submit to its rules? (Colossians 2:20, *NIV*).

The question is, *Why are we living in the world and submitting ourselves to the decrees of poverty, sickness and death that we have been redeemed from?* If we have died with Christ and have been raised with Him and seated with Him in heavenly places, then the elementary principles of the world do not dictate to us.

We have been made whole and complete! Only the devil wants us to believe that we cannot live in completeness. He doesn't want us to believe that we were created to be well.

We've got to keep looking up, seeking the things above, so that we have the heavenly perspective of those raised with Him. Colossians 3:2 says, "Set your mind on the things above, not on the things that are on earth." We have to come to a place where we set our mind on the Word of truth that is unshakeable, not on the things of the earth.

Redeemed with His Fullness

We can have completion, because the blood of the lamb has cleansed "us from *all* unrighteousness" (1 John 1:9), including sickness.

We need to know the depth of love that Jesus had for us in order for Him to go to the cross on our behalf. It surpasses knowledge. And it surpasses our understanding to know that we can be filled up with that same love—full of all the fullness of God. If we're filled up with the fullness of God, then there won't be any room for sin or sickness.

In Him you have been made complete (Colossians 2:10).

Second Corinthians 4:7 states, "We have this treasure in earthen vessels, so that the surpassing greatness of the power will be of God and not from ourselves." We have a treasure from God: the surpassing greatness of His power. It's that power that puts us into a proper place, and this isn't based on what we believe in ourselves but on what God says. The power is miraculous power. The verse says that the surpassing greatness of the miraculous power of God is *within us*. And it is a power that is able to overcome sickness.

When we take our proper position of completeness, then we become the Body of Jesus.

Blessed is the Lord God of Israel, for He has visited and redeemed His people (Luke 1:68, *NKJV*).

The word "redeemed" in the passage above means "bought back" or "debt paid off." Redemption gives completion. If the debt was purchased, if the fall of man was paid for on the cross, if Jesus bought up sin and sickness, then why would we want to pay for it ourselves? He purchased it so that we wouldn't have to pay for it.

Deliverance from sin is a state of being redeemed. When we're in a state of redemption, then we're in a condition where we no longer embrace sin and sickness. When we get into a proper position, heaven lines up with us and all hell is broken off of us. Sure, there will be attacks. The enemy doesn't like it when we gain this level of understanding of truth. But the enemy doesn't have authority over us; the truth of the Word of God does.

IMMUNIZED BY REDEMPTION

It's important that we understand exactly what redemption has redeemed us from. There is an important connection between *being redeemed* and *having the armor of God*. Redemption sets us free from the law of sin and death. It puts protection around believers, providing us with an *immune system* from sin and death. An immune system helps protect the body from pathogens, or disease-producing agents like viruses and bacteria.

We also have a spiritual immunity—a protection from disease—that comes through redemption. If we've been redeemed from sickness, then we need to be free from the punishment (which Jesus bore so that we wouldn't have to). Redemption is our immune system, protecting us from sickness and disease.

An antibody is something the body produces to act as a defense against foreign and/or harmful substances; antibodies help immune systems. God's will produces an immune system within believers. That's our armor. It is a defense against what the enemy tries to do to us.

An antigen is a substance that stimulates the production of antibodies. God's plan calls for *faith* to be the substance "of things hoped for," the evidence "of things not seen" (Hebrews 11:1). Isaiah 10:27 says, "The yoke shall be destroyed because of the anointing" (*KJV*). In other words, the anointing is God's antigen that stimulates the production of an immune system within the believer, and it is activated by faith in the truth of the Word of God.

Immunity is the state of being resistant to disease. Immunity is the condition that permits either natural or acquired resistance to disease. We acquire resistance through redemption. The whole idea of being immune through redemption is knowing that redemption brings us to a place of recovering what was lost. It's a buyback. We're set free by the payment of a ransom. We're brought back to a proper order. We're rescued from sin. In other words, Jesus redeemed us, which puts us back to the proper position (before the Fall): a place where there is no sin or sickness in the Body of Christ.

Protected by God's Armor

"Finally, be strong in the Lord and in the strength of His might. Put on the full armor of God, so that you will be able to stand firm against the schemes of the devil" (Ephesians 6:10-11). In this verse, Paul says that we are to be strong in Jesus. That's why we put on His armor: to stand in the strength of His might. That's a place where we stand firm against any attack of sickness that comes from the enemy's camp.

> Stand firm therefore, having girded your loins with truth, and having put on the breastplate of righteousness, and having shod your feet with the preparation of the gospel of peace; in addition to all, taking up the shield of faith with which you will be able to extinguish all the flaming arrows of the evil one. And take the helmet of salvation, and the sword of the Spirit, which is the word of God (Ephesians 6:14-17).

This is the armor of God that Paul tells us to don:

- *Truth*—Because it contains evidence of divine health
- *Righteousness*—Because redemption redeemed us into that place
- *Peace*—Because perfect peace is ours when our eyes are fixed on Jesus
- *Faith*—Because our faith brings what God has to us.
- *Salvation*—Because we step into divine health once we step into the redemptive value that Jesus bestows

upon us ("Salvation" refers to deliverance or being in a state of health.)

- *The Word of God*—Because this is the sword that we have to swing and cut away the attacks of the enemy, giving us power to overcome the devil

A change in condition may not happen overnight. We may have to work to embrace the proper position of the truth about divine healing and have our mind renewed to it. Looking to the Word and believing it fervently and unquestioningly, and then living it out in our lives, as we listen to and obey the Holy Spirit's voice, are what leads us into the realm of divine health.

8

THE *Apostolic* GENERATION

There is coming in the Body of Christ a new apostolic reformation. God is maturing the Church into the fullness of Christ, and the household of God must pursue the perfection that this fullness will bring.

Jesus tells us in Colossians 2:10 that we have been made complete. That completeness occurs when the Church becomes the righteousness of Christ. God wants the Church to be united in order that the Body of Christ will begin to fulfill the Great Commission of going into our cities and bringing forth a revival around the world. He wants to move us from a rapture mentality into a harvest theology. For that to happen, we must move away from a spirit of religion and into a spirit of revelation.

According to Ephesians 2:20, the early apostles and prophets, along with Christ as the cornerstone, laid a foundation upon which the house of God is built. The Church has neglected that foundation and must get back to it. Parts of the foundation are cracked, and other parts have been completely torn down. Present-day apostles and prophets must begin to repair that foundation of truth. Without it, we cannot live a victorious life.

THE THIRD-DAY CHURCH

A house is not built on a foundation of unbelief. Many in the Church have lost belief that the work of the Holy Spirit is relevant to the building up of believers. We prevent ourselves from operating in the fruits and gifts of the Holy Spirit when we don't believe they are for today. We need them now just as much as believers needed them in the first century.

I see a new revival taking place, a stirring in the Body of Christ that will begin to reveal a truth about healing: God is not merely *able* to heal us, but He also *wants* to! This revelation will take us beyond healing to the point where we will begin pursuing the realm of divine health.

A Third-Day church is being raised up in this day. Hosea 6:2 says, "After two days he will revive us; on the third day he will restore us, that we may live in his presence" (*NIV*). The end-time church must come to a place where we are pursuing the face of God, where we are in the presence of God and the glory of God, a place where the great anointing for signs and wonders and healings and miracles will take place.

A Third-Day church is not just an end-time church that is stirred up in day two but one that begins to pursue God in day three, as the prophet Hosea said.

The Day Has Arrived

Second Peter 3:8 says, "With the Lord one day is like a thousand years and a thousand years like one day." If from the beginning to A.D. 1000 was the first day and from 1000 to 2000 was the second day, then in 2001 we entered the third day. This is now the Third-Day church; and it will begin to move into the presence of God. It will pursue His face rather than His hand. It will pursue the Healer rather than the healing. It will get hold of the things of God and begin to obey Him in all areas.

In day two, before the year 2000, we saw the great end-time revivals: the Azusa Street Revival, the Welsh Revival, the Brownsville Revival, the Toronto Revival. The reviving of the Church is a reviving of the Body of Christ to bring us to a place where we are more desperate for Jesus than we are for our own life.

Old things are passing away and things are being cast off the Body of Christ that have caused us to walk in form but not to walk in power. We will now begin to have an understanding that God has a fire He wants burning within each of us that will cause us to forge ahead and not retreat; to have a desire to see the end-time harvest taken; to develop a burden to pursue the lost in our cities; and to realize that God wants us to reap the final harvest so that we can partake in the wedding of the Lamb.

We need that fire in the end-time, Third-Day church. There's a stirring across the land. When we march forward across this bridge to God, the bridge will catch fire behind us so that we can't go back—and we're not willing to go back, because that old-time religion just isn't going to cut it anymore, not with the fire of God in our bones!

When John the Baptist came, he said:

As for me, I baptize you with water for repentance, but He who is coming after me is mightier than I, and I am not fit to remove His sandals; He will baptize you with the Holy Spirit and fire (Matthew 3:11).

It's time that the Church gets the fire. The Third-Day church will be the one that receives that fire of God, that face-to-face encounter that results from pursuing His face. The Church will be so stirred that they will have a hunger that won't quit and a fire that will not be quenched until God's will be done.

God's Lightning Will Come

The original Greek word for what is translated as "fire" in Matthew 3:11 is also used to refer to lightning; thus, we can think of the lightning of God beginning to come into us.

The Scripture goes on to say:

His winnowing fork is in His hand, and He will thoroughly clear His threshing floor; and He will gather His wheat into the barn, but He will burn up the chaff with unquenchable fire (Matthew 3:12).

"Winnowing fork is in his hand" reveals God as a *refiner*. He refines the visible Church, which is His threshing floor. This separation of the wheat from the chaff refers to the separation of the flesh from the Spirit so that we won't move in form; we will move in power. We won't move by religion; we will move by revelation.

We will receive this fire because our God is a *consuming fire* whose Word will make His ministers flames of fire. We are to become that fire. We are to be stirred up, for God is going to cleanse the threshing floor and purge the Church, His Body, of the unregenerate. A Church of obedient believers will then receive the Spirit beyond measure.

This is all about wrapping up and binding up the visible Church. When God says, "He will gather His wheat into the barn," that barn is the garnering spot—the place where completion will come into the Body of Christ. It's a place (God's house) where the wheat is separated from the chaff and where God "will burn up the chaff with unquenchable fire." "Unquenchable" is translated from a Greek word that means perpetual, so this means that God's fire is the kind of fire that will not go out—ever.

If you've ever observed people at a revival or personally experienced a renewal, you've probably noticed that the people have a fire in them that cannot be put out. They burn for Jesus. They can't go back to where they were because they are now in a place where they have received a baptism of fire that has given them an unending passion in their heart. This is the attitude of the Third-Day church. We believers are pursuing the face of God. And the things of God are coming to us because what God has for us comes to us when we get into the presence of a heavenly Father who desires to give us all He has.

Hebrews 6 talks about perfection. God's desire is that the Third-Day church will come into a place of perfection, a place where it begins to receive all that God is:

> Therefore leaving the elementary teaching about the Christ, let us press on to maturity, not laying again a foundation of repentance from dead works and of faith toward God, of instruction about washings and laying on of hands, and the resurrection of the dead and eternal judgment (Hebrews 6:1-2).

God is telling us to *move on!* Ephesians 2:20 talks about the foundation laid by the early apostles. God wants us to begin to build the Church on that foundation with current-day apostles, to begin to perfect the Church and lay in these doctrines that put the Church into a place of maturity where we begin to understand that we are not to just be *hearers* of the Word but also *doers* of the Word. That doing requires us to have a vision to see a great harvest taken.

The Six Hebrews 6 Doctrines Will Be Fulfilled

There are six doctrines mentioned in Hebrews 6:1-2: (1) repentance from dead works, (2) faith in God, (3) baptism, (4) laying on of hands, (5) resurrection of the dead, and (6) eternal judgment. These six doctrines *perfect* the Church. Many of them have already been fulfilled in the end-time church. Let's take a look at each of them:

1. *Repentance from dead works* was re-emphasized in the Church in the sixteenth century through Martin Luther. He stressed that a person must come to Christ personally through faith and repentance of sins.

2. *Faith in God* was re-emphasized in the Church through the Holiness Movement. The Body of Christ began to focus on the fact that the Word of God produces faith in the believer and that without faith, we cannot please God (see Hebrews 11:6).

3. *Baptism* was re-emphasized in the Church in the 1900s by the giftings that began to manifest in believers

through the baptism of the Holy Spirit, including the gift of speaking in other tongues. This emphasis came through Charles Parham, William Seymour, the Azusa Street Revival and the Pentecostal movement, among others.

4. *The laying on of hands* was re-emphasized in the Church through the healing evangelists of the Latter Rain movement in the 1940s and '50s. At that time, the Latter Rain movement began the fivefold ministry: the administrative offices of apostles, profits, pastors, teachers and evangelists. This doctrine taught us that these gifts were for the perfecting of the saints until the Church reaches a unity of faith (see Ephesians 4:11).

5. *The resurrection of the dead* must come through the end-time church, which receives the fire of God, has a separation of the flesh and spirit, and is in the presence and anointing of God, from whom comes the greatest power: the raising of the dead.

6. *Eternal judgment* will come when God decides where our soul will reside, and this will affect every single person who has ever taken a breath on planet Earth.

REVELATION RELATIONSHIP

When the Word of God comes to the believer, it will inspire one of two things: *religion* (which will have a tendency to keep you where you are) or *revelation* (which will begin to move you to where God wants you to be).

The spirit of religion is a spirit that comes from the enemy's camp. It is a spirit that will cause someone to strap on a bomb and set it off on a bus full of innocent victims. It is a spirit that causes some Christians to sit in a pew for 10 years in a church and be no further along in their relationship with God than when they first sat in that pew.

Revelation reveals something by the Holy Spirit so that we can move from being merely a hearer to being a doer. We can't do something that we're not aware of or we don't know about. Revelation communicates something to the Church that the Church can use to begin to establish the will of God as the Holy Spirit reveals what His will is.

It is vitally important that we understand the value of pursuing the revelation of the Holy Spirit, as Paul commanded in 1 Corinthians 14:1: "Follow the way of love and eagerly desire spiritual gifts, especially the gift of prophecy" (*NIV*). It bears repeating that the spirit of revelation is not something you get; it's *Someone* you know. Revelation comes through a relationship with the Holy Spirit, who will lead the believer in all the truth that the Father has (see John 16:13-15). The value of revelation is in the fulfillment of the will of God *in* and *through* the believer so that the kingdom of God can come on the earth. Revelation uncovers the will of God so that it is understood spiritually—not with the mind of man, but through the *spirit* of man.

Remember that James 1:8 says that "a double-minded man [is] unstable in all his ways." We become double-minded or unstable when we try to use our mind in conjunction with or instead of the mind of Christ (see 1 Corinthians 2:16). That doesn't work. We cannot process the Word of God with our finite, human mind. It must be processed spirit to spirit, which gives us the mind of Christ through the Holy Spirit (as we cast down the imaginings of our mind).

The Mindset of Christ

First Corinthians 2:16 tells us that "we have the mind of Christ." The reason we have the mind of Christ is that He is our Head. The mind of Christ is the spirit of revelation. The whole idea of God connecting us, raising us and seating us in heavenly places with Jesus is to connect us with the Head (Jesus). Once the connection is made, God fills us with the same Holy Spirit that raised Jesus so that there will be a revelation to us of the mind of Christ.

If we want to know what the mind of Christ Jesus is, then we need to get ourselves into the will of God. We must get into the Word of God and allow the Holy Spirit to reveal truth in that Word. His truth will set us completely free of all misunderstanding, of the paralysis of inactivity, of sickness, of lack, of worry and of fear.

Ever notice that we get into the most trouble when we think of our own selves? God is trying to get us to *stop thinking* apart from Him, and to surrender our thoughts to the mind of Christ. Revelation moves us beyond what we could ask or think in the natural with our mind (see Ephesians 3:20), and we can begin to think with the mind of Christ as the Holy Spirit reveals it to us.

Ephesians 4:17 talks about walking "in the futility" of our mind. In our mind, in the natural, we have futility. We read one thing and believe and live another because revelation hasn't revealed something (since we don't believe it or because it doesn't fit our experiences). Then we try to bring the Word of God down to the level of our experiences rather than having our experiences raised *up* to His Word.

God wants to renew our mind. He wants it to be *renewed*, not *conformed*, to the world. He wants us and the world transformed by the Holy Spirit. Our mind will cause us to dwell on the past; His mind will cause us to look to the future. In other words, as we begin processing the will of God, we begin to alter the course of our life, impacting our future and putting us into proper alignment with the will of God.

The Spirit of Religion

Religion will cause us to stop being God-sensitive and make us seeker sensitive, by tailoring our message so that it doesn't offend those who are curious (rather than those who are serious) about God. A seeker-sensitive religiosity leads us to want things to fit what we desire rather than what God desires. When we move in a spirit of religion, we have a tendency to make living our own life our top priority. We sit in a church pew just to get over the mess we've accumulated all week long.

A spirit of religion also deludes us into believing that the devil has the power to make us sick. We live all bound up because we don't realize that we have power over the enemy. We don't understand that God (who has far more power than Satan) can easily make us well. We're bound up justifying the way we are rather than pursuing the way we ought to be. And we explain away why we're sick rather than knowing why we're healed: because God desires His children to be well!

If we're all bound up like that, then maybe we're living by the belief system of the enemy. The chains of bondage have been broken in heaven, but if we're living under a false system of religious ritual, then we are blocking the release of God's full power into our life. We can't get set free when we're living in the past. The past leads us to believe more in what the devil did yesterday than to believe what God is doing to bless us today and tomorrow. All that thinking causes us to latch on to someone else's faith rather than growing in faith in God's infallible Word ourselves.

We can choose to reject the power of the enemy—he only wants to limit us. We must assert our authority in the Kingdom—God gave it to us!

Our Unlimited Authority of Power

In the Cascade Mountains outside of the city of Spokane, Washington, there's an imaginary boundary called the snake line. When you're hiking in the mountains *above* the snake line, you can't get bitten (supposedly, snakes don't live at elevations higher than this line).

Too much of the Body of Christ today is living below the snake line—and they wonder why they're going around getting bitten all the time! What they don't realize is that in Christ, they possess unlimited power to live above the line all the time.

Limits create fences, which prevent our escape. Our enemy limits us with our past so that he can fence in our future, which causes us to allow God only limited access to our life. Then the Holy Spirit can't reveal truth to us. Revelation can't come, because we're processing heaven by the limited standards of Earth.

But the kingdom of God has no limits. We can do *all things* through Christ (see Philippians 4:13)—we have authority over all of it! When revelation reveals truth, we are set free, because truth never looks back; *truth moves forward.* And this is truth: We have a future that doesn't look anything like our past! But we can't be released from something we're hanging on to. We must allow the Holy Spirit to reveal to us that we *can* choose to release our past and not have it bind up our future.

The enemy has apparently had quite a bit of success in wanting us to have a religious mindset that causes us to continue to accept sickness that Jesus already vanquished, paid for and settled by His payment on the cross. The miraculous resides in our future, not in our past. Our past is our Egypt. We must be willing to cross over our Jordan River, reach forward into the Canaan land of our deliverance and take possession of the unlimited power given us by Christ. In Him, we can live beyond what the enemy does. Sure, a war will take place, for we battle, not against flesh and blood, but against evil principalities and wicked strongholds (see Ephesians 6:12). But remember, Luke 10:19 tells us that we have "authority . . . over all the power of the enemy." There's a place in God where we have absolute authority, where we have the power to tear down strongholds, where we become the victorious Bride of Christ against whom no weapon formed can prosper (see Isaiah 54:17).

The Pharisees taught that man should serve the law. But Jesus taught that the *law should serve man* (see Mark 2:27). The letter of the law kills, because it has no life. Religion wants us to live by the letter so that we can never quite fully believe we've been redeemed.

Jesus said, "The kingdom of God is at hand" (Mark 1:15). He didn't say it is beyond our reach; He said it's "at hand"—it's *within us* (see Luke 17:21). If it's within us, then we can reach it—indeed, we *have* reached it. The things of God are in the realm of God, the supernatural realm, to which, by the Holy Spirit in us, we have direct access. But we can't access something in the supernatural realm of God until we learn to operate in that realm. Likewise, we cannot see what is to come until we learn to see what hasn't yet come. To do that, we must begin to have a revelation of the supernatural realm that is available to the believer *right now*.

Our Transformation by Revelation

When the Word of God doesn't take us to an encounter with God, all it does is produce more religion in us. But God is not looking for more of the same; He's looking to *transform us* with revelation.

Revelation will cause us to begin to process the things of heaven here on the earth so that the kingdom of God that is within us can begin to flow through our life and out into the world.

In Romans 12:2, we are told, "Do not be conformed to this world, but be transformed by the renewing of your mind, so that you may prove what the will of God is, that which is good and acceptable and perfect." But we can't prove the will of God with a milquetoast mindset. We can't prove His will if we don't believe we have His power through the Holy Spirit in us. In order to prove the will of God, there must be a demonstration of the power of God—a transformation by revelation.

Our Mind of Christ

"The mind set on the flesh leads to death, but the mind set on the Spirit is life and peace" (Romans 8:6). When our mind is set on the Spirit, the Spirit gives us life and peace, and we no longer fear the enemy or the world.

Fear causes past trauma to be a present reality.

Fear becomes the substance of what we do not want.

Fear causes lack of revelation of the truth that we can move beyond fear and into the peace of God.

As Proverbs 23:7 says, we are what we think: "For as he thinks within himself, so he is." Revelation causes us to think God-conscious thoughts:

> *I am the Body of Christ.*
> *I have authority.*
> *I am mighty in God for tearing down strongholds.*
> *I am not subject to the enemy; he is subject to me.*

Past personal trauma doesn't have to affect our future. That's why 2 Corinthians 10:5 says for us to cast down imaginings and those things that exalt themselves "against the knowledge of God." They are a lying vanity that the enemy brings when we operate in a religious mindset.

When we have the mind of Christ, we see what Jesus sees. We can see heaven better than we can see Earth. We have a heavenly perspective of the world. Our mind is renewed to heaven rather than conformed to Earth. With the mind of Christ, we walk in utter faith.

But the spirit of religion cuts faith off. When a religious spirit gains a stronghold, we become deaf to the spirit of the Word. The spirit of religion causes us to no longer hear what the Spirit is saying, and then we can't do what the Word requires of us. This keeps us where we are, making us inflexible, disallowing growth, cutting off revelation.

The spirit of religion is pervasive in a church when it has spread throughout every part of the church. If left alone long enough, this pervasive spirit becomes a *perverse* spirit, turning us from good to immoral. A perverse spirit becomes obstinate, opposing what is right. The tongue can no longer be a creative force (see Proverbs 18:21). When we no longer speak the truth of the Word, then we can no longer activate it in our life. When we can't activate it, we can't be set free. The result is that when we cannot move in God's unseen realm, we begin to lack confidence in God and in His Word.

So will My word be which goes forth from My mouth;
it will not return to Me empty, without accomplishing
what I desire, and without succeeding in the matter for
which I sent it (Isaiah 55:11).

The religious spirit will prevent the Word from accomplishing anything in our life. Without truth revealed, everything is *impossible* to the believer, because this spirit only operates by sight and not by faith. When our spiritual hearing is blocked, faith can't move us; we only go by what we see rather than by what we hear in the spiritual realm. Then we can only operate in the natural realm, where little faith is required. Our confession then lines up with the earthly realm, becoming something like, "Well, gosh, I prayed for him, but I didn't see any change. I guess he wasn't healed." Or, "I received prayer, but I don't feel any different. I reckon it didn't happen." Without faith, the will of God simply cannot move in our life.

The Spirit of the Pharisee

A spirit of religion becomes a pharisaical spirit that provides only an explanation, not a solution. This spirit causes people to say things like, "Well, God made me sick to teach me something." Or they claim, "God will heal me sometime—if it's His will." Or they say, "God is sovereign. He can do what He wants. If He wanted me well, I would be well."

Luke 6 tells about how Jesus healed a man with a withered hand and how the Pharisees reacted to the miracle: "They themselves were filled with rage, and discussed together what they might do to Jesus" (v. 11). The Pharisees were standing strictly on the law and completely ignored the fact that a man with a lifelong physical deformity had just been miraculously healed before their very eyes! To them, keeping the law was more important than healing the precious, hurting people. They were so caught up in a legalistic spirit that they didn't just miss the miracle, they missed the miracle worker Himself—the very Messiah the Jews had been expecting for centuries!

Even when Jesus corrected their faulty interpretation of the law when He asked them, "Is it lawful to do good or to do harm on the Sabbath, to save a life or to destroy it?" (Luke 6:9), they didn't even respond to His question.

A Religion of Tradition

The religious spirit of the Pharisees became tradition and caused them to completely miss the miracles that God had for them. This is the type of spirit that will cause a Christian to go to a hospital and hold the hand of a sick person until the person dies rather than lay hands on the sick and boldly proclaim in the name of Jesus, "Rise up and walk!"

Tradition can completely invalidate God's Word, as Jesus tells us:

Thus invalidating the word of God by your tradition which you have handed down; and you do many things such as that (Mark 7:13).

The spirit of religion will cause us to be overly influenced by tradition, bringing us to an attitude that says, "Well, this is our tradition—this is the way we always do it." Revelation, on the other hand, brings constant growth.

Tradition has a tendency to lock God in a box, preventing people from moving in Christ. The spirit of religion becomes a controlling spirit, rendering everything around us impossible to deal with in a manner that glorifies God.

The spirit of religion causes us to be double-minded. When we are double-minded, our circumstances cause us to question God (see James 1:6-8). Rather than lining up with God, we try to make God line up with us. If the spirit of religion is upon a believer, that believer can't approach God in faith, because what the Spirit is saying (and faith comes only by hearing) can't be heard, as Romans 10:17 says. This believer is driven and tossed by circumstances (see James 1:5-8). This believer is double-minded because he or she reads one thing in the Word and believes another from the world. If our circumstances, our tradition, our religion, cause us to doubt, then our foundation was never set solidly in the Word of God in the first place.

Double-mindedness causes us to tune out. Then, as Jesus said, we can no longer hear the Word: "Why do you not understand what I am saying? It is because you cannot hear My word" (John 8:43).

When this spirit of religion is pervasive, it causes what I call "a spirit of stupid." I use "stupid" here to mean *numb* or *very dull in mind*. If people have a spirit of stupid, they are in a stupor or in a state of extreme apathy.

Hebrews 4:12 says, "The word of God is living and active and sharper than any two-edged sword." With a religious spirit, when we swing our sword, nothing seems to get cut away. This is because we've lost our sharpness. When we are dull, our sword is dull.

> The heart of this people has become dull, with their ears they scarcely hear, and they have closed their eyes, otherwise they would see with their eyes, hear with their ears, and understand with their heart and return, and I would heal them (Matthew 13:15; see also Acts 28:27).

When we scarcely hear, we just get enough of God to make us miserable, because in our spirit we know we aren't going the distance for Him—not even halfway. When we're dull and feeling completely hung out or suspended, we can't get anywhere. It's like driving with our brakes on.

> Concerning him we have much to say, and it is hard to explain, since you have become dull of hearing. For though by this time you ought to be teachers, you have

need again for someone to teach you the elementary principles of the oracles of God, and you have come to need milk and not solid food. For everyone who partakes only of milk is not accustomed to the word of righteousness, for he is an infant. But solid food is for the mature, who because of practice have their senses trained to discern good and evil (Hebrews 5:11-14).

Milk keeps us in infancy, where we require constant care. We have to grow to maturity so that we can learn to tell the difference between good and evil (see Hebrews 5:14). To grow into maturity, we have to practice the solid meat of the Word so that we will develop and strengthen as followers of God. We're not babies anymore—He wants us off the religious milk!

Overcoming the Spirit of Religion

So how do we break the spirit of religion? We break it by having our ears truly open to what the Word is saying, *and* by then obeying it:

> The Lord God has given me his words of wisdom so that I may know what I should say to all these weary ones. Morning by morning he wakens me and opens my understanding to his will. The Lord God has spoken to me and I have listened; I do not rebel nor turn away (Isaiah 50:4-5, *TLB*).

When the spirit of religion is broken, our ears can open and we can receive the revelation of the Holy Spirit:

On that day the deaf will hear words of a book, and out of their gloom and darkness the eyes of the blind will see. The afflicted also will increase their gladness in the LORD, and the needy of mankind will rejoice in the Holy One of Israel (Isaiah 29:18-19).

"On that day the deaf shall hear words of a book" means to speak and bring forth what is in the Word. "The afflicted" refers to the depressed in mind or in circumstances. Notice that this passage doesn't say that the deaf will hear sound—they can hear just fine in the natural—but now they will begin to hear in the supernatural and be set free.

GOD'S GOVERNMENT

God's desire is to bring forth an apostolic government through the Body of Christ. Then we can begin to overlay His kingdom onto cities so that the government of man can be overlaid by the government of God, and His kingdom can then be established in cities around the world.

Isaiah 9:6 says that "the government will rest" on the shoulders of Jesus. We are the Body of Christ, and Jesus is our Head. Because we are His Body, the government is on our shoulders. If the government were to remain on Jesus' shoulders and He were to do this work, then it would have already been completed by now. But because of our free will, He puts it upon our shoulders and then gives us authority to bring forth that government and put it into effect. It's all up to us.

Isaiah 9:7 adds, "There will be no end to the increase of His government." It will continue to increase to the end of the age, in parameters and offices set in place by Jesus Himself:

> He gave some as apostles, and some as prophets, and some as evangelists, and some as pastors and teachers, for the equipping of the saints for the work of service, to the building up of the body of Christ (Ephesians 4:11-12).

Part of His government includes a fivefold ministry in the church. This is why there is a new apostolic movement in the end-time, the Third-Day church. There will not be a threefold ministry (pastors, teachers and evangelists) but a *fivefold* ministry (apostles, prophets, pastors, teachers and evangelists). The fivefold ministry releases the five senses into the church. The five senses cause us to hear what the Spirit is saying. They cause us to see the vision God gives the Body of Christ. They cause us to touch the sick and see them healed.

The early apostles and prophets talked about in the New Testament laid the foundation. But over the ages, as mentioned earlier, the Church has torn down different parts of that foundation; and it's the restoration of the foundation that current-day apostles and prophets must begin. One part of that restoration is the work of healing in the Church. But it must come from the fivefold ministry. Ephesians 4:13 adds, "*Until* we all attain to the unity of the faith" (emphasis added). Until we attain to that unity, we need apostles, prophets, pastors, teachers and evangelists working together so that the Church can become a mature

Church, perfected to move in power. Otherwise, we live in a "Sunday mindset": We just visit the local church for an hour each week, while the devil is busy 24/7 messing up our cities.

The devil loves "church in a box" for an hour a week. That kind of church is no threat to him. It's when the Church gets out of the box and begins to have a vision for the city that the people of God will become a threat to the enemy's camp.

City Transformation

Our vision must be bigger than the front door of a church. Our vision must be as big as the city. We must realize that the Holy Spirit is capable of transforming entire cities. The local church has a right not to embrace apostles and prophets until apostles and prophets learn to work together to restore the foundation back to the Church. It does no good for a prophet to come into a city and release a prophecy if there isn't an apostolic work to carry it through. In order to see a city transformed, the local church needs to see the benefit of apostles and prophets working together to establish a vision and then working together to draw the Body of Christ into that vision. When we do that, the local church will be added to daily by a harvesting army bringing the city to Christ. Then the local church will become an equipping center to release the warriors back out into the city so that the great end-time harvest can take place.

> [We] are of God's household, having been built on the foundation of the apostles and prophets, Christ Jesus Himself being the corner stone, in whom the whole building, being fitted together, is growing into

a holy temple in the Lord, in whom you also are being built together into a dwelling of God in the Spirit (Ephesians 2:19-22).

We are the house of God, His dwelling place. The house is built upon a foundation of apostles and prophets, and it needs to be solid with not just an apostolic foundation and not just a prophetic foundation. The two must work together so that the prophet will hear from God and proclaim what is heard, and the apostle will begin to bring the people of God together and initiate the building.

Apostles

Second Corinthians 12:12 states plainly that the things that mark an apostle are "signs and wonders and miracles." Apostles are not people who just show up with "Apostle" written on a business card. Apostles are people who are recognized because of the fruit of the work they do. Apostles are people who move in a spirit of humility, not seeking attention for themselves, as Paul says in 1 Corinthians 4:10-13. They are people who equip and release the saints. Apostles build the Body of Christ, bringing believers into a place of maturity. They work with prophets, pastors, teachers and evangelists. Apostles bring unity into the Body of Christ.

Apostles will have vision for the harvest. Because of their humility, they will have the heart of a servant who rules and reigns with the King yet serves the people. Apostles will edify and build up the Body of Christ. They will have a vision to see a city transformed and to see the Bride of Christ united in that vision—and the Body working together to bring it about. The heart of every apostle is to usher in the kingdom of God, for it is His kingdom that fulfills the will of God on Earth.

One Vision

The Lord gave me a vision of the Bride of Christ coming out of the harvest field and into the wedding chamber. But the Bride did not have a wedding gown on—not yet. She had the armor of God, and she was a *fivefold* bride.

When I viewed her, she was covered with golden armor. Over her helmet was the word "Victory." On her breastplate were the words "Well done, good and faithful servant." She carried a golden sword. When I looked upon this Bride, her faceplate had no eye slits.

I asked, "Holy Spirit, why is it she has no eye slits?"

He answered, "Because this Bride was not to walk by sight; she was to walk by every word that proceeded out of the mouth of God."

She was the Bride of Christ who had a vision that was unending, a Bride in victory. No longer a victim, she moved in the authority God had given her.

That is the apostolic coming. That is the government of God on its way.

THE APOSTOLIC PEOPLE

Apostolic people are those who will begin to embrace and come under the fivefold ministry of the Church. They will be a people who will become fathers to a fatherless generation.

When we come into *covenant*, we're not covenanting with a pastor or an apostle; we're covenanting with what God is doing *in* the pastor or the apostle. We're coming into a covenant relationship that causes us to give our life to what God is doing. When we give our life to what God is doing as evidenced by the manifestation of the fruit of our work, then we have the gifts that we desire—because God's will becomes our will. The dreams we desire are released in that covenant relationship, because apostles equip and release.

The goal of the Third-Day church movement in the end-time church is to release the dreams and the hopes of the Bride of Christ so that she can come into fullness and become all that God has called her to be as she submits her life to what Jesus is doing in end-time apostolic works.

God is raising up an apostolic generation in the Third-Day church. The Church is coming to a place in God where believers no longer seek His hand; they seek His face. They're moving in absolute authority and power. They are moved by the spirit of revelation. They will demonstrate God's power. They will constantly pursue all that God is and has. They will heal the sick. They will raise the dead. They'll realize that healing the sick and raising the dead is the *normal* operation of the Church. This end-time army of God will bring the fulfillment of His will with the demonstration of power.

Miracles are not out of our reach; they are only out of our sight. Revelation establishes vision so that the will of God can be seen and understood and so that miracles will return to our everyday sight, as it was in the first century.

The only thing between the unseen and the seen realm is you and me. The only limits God has are *us*.

9

Healing THE LAND

LOSS OF STEWARDSHIP

Sin defiles us as well as the land we have stewardship over (see Ezra 9:11; Leviticus 18:25-28; 2 Samuel 21:1-2,14; Revelation 18:5). The fall of man opened the door for sickness to attack our bodies *and* our land. Thus, we not only need to have healing for the Body of Christ, but we also need healing for the land (see 2 Chronicles 7:14).

Genesis 1:28 says that God gave man "dominion over" the earth (*NKJV*). God created man in His image and placed him on the land. All the provision man needed was made available on the land that God gave man to rule over. When Adam fell, he lost stewardship over that which God gave him to enjoy. And since Adam had dominion over the earth, when he fell, so did the earth. The earth then became subject to the sin of man:

> For the creation was subjected to futility, not willingly, but because of Him who subjected it in hope; because the creation itself also will be delivered from the bondage of corruption into the glorious liberty of the children of God (Romans 8:20-21, *NKJV*).

Loss of stewardship comes through defilement. According to Romans 8:22, all creation now "groans" for the humanity to be restored to its proper place of dominion over the land. This groaning was ushered in by the fall of humankind through Adam and Eve's choice to sin. In other words, we were cursed because of the choice to deliberately disobey God. However, in Deuteronomy 28:2 we are told we can be blessed again *if* we simply follow God's law.

The blessings of obedience are many. Obeying God brings blessing in our cities, in the nation, in our bodies, with the produce of our ground, with an increase of our cattle and with an increase of food. We are blessed because our enemy will be defeated. We are blessed because we will have an increase in our storehouse. We are blessed because everything we set our hands to will become a blessing.

THE RESULT OF DEFILEMENT

But it's a quid pro quo: When we disobey God, we lose those blessings. We become cursed and the land becomes defiled because of our immorality and worshiping idols rather than God.

Under the curse, the land begins to die. When we disobey God, we lose the provision that the land gives us. We lose the food supply. The air becomes foul and polluted. Water quality degrades. Weather changes produce drought. The forest is lost, and the animals on the earth can no longer be sustained. Then come wars, and with them, disease, hunger and increased crime rates.

Sin separates us from God, and we no longer reflect the identity He gave us as His children. Families begin to break down. Moral standards decline. What was right becomes wrong, and what was wrong in God's sight becomes right in ours. We are led by the flesh, and standards of morality based on personal desires instead of God's standards are established. Like frogs in slowly boiling water, society increasingly declines . . . until death.

If you are living according to the flesh, you must die (Romans 8:13).

Here is how the great prophet Isaiah describes this decline of humankind:

All of us have become like one who is unclean, and all our righteous acts are like filthy rags; we all shrivel up like a leaf, and like the wind our sins sweep us away (Isaiah 64:6, *NIV*).

Even what we consider "righteous acts" in our blinded moral state, God says "are like filthy rags." Isaiah 59:2 says that our iniquities have separated us from God, and our sins have caused Him to hide His face from us, and He will not hear us. We cannot hear from God, and God will not hear from us.

VISION FOR OUR CITIES

God wants to give us a vision for how to get our cities redeemed from the curse of defilement. Galatians 3:14 explains why Christ redeemed us from the curse of the law: "in order that in Christ

Jesus the blessing of Abraham might come to the Gentiles." If God has the power to heal the Body of Jesus and bring the blessings of Abraham to us, then through the Holy Spirit within us, the Body has the power to redeem cities.

When Healing Rooms Ministries conducted a recent International Spiritual Hunger Conference in Spokane, Cindy Jacobs was one of our speakers. God gave her a message that He intended to join healing of the Body with healing of the land. Cindy released that message to us, and we received an understanding that the healing of the land is the Body of Christ being healed and that pursuing the harvest is what brings about a transformed city. We were given an understanding that the power of the Holy Spirit is strong enough to heal a city.

The Bible says that a nation can be taken in a day (see Isaiah 66:8), so we knew that healing could come to an entire city. But we weren't sure how this was going to happen. Then the Holy Spirit began to talk to me, saying, "I'm going to show you how I can redeem a city. I'm going to put a steel punch into the darkest place of the city of Spokane."

At that time, the darkest place in Spokane was called Sprague Avenue. Sprague Avenue had become home to topless bars, prostitution and drug dealing. It was a very dark place. Places like that are established by the sins of our ancestors. It was the forefathers of Spokane who had brought defilement to the land by allowing those activities to take place and thus had laid the foundation for subsequent generations to live in that defilement.

But the Holy Spirit said to me, "I'm going to show you how I can put a *steel punch* into the darkest place of the city and begin to bring healing into it." A steel punch is something that I had read about in a book written by Israeli general Moshe Dayan. He wrote about an ingenious plan he devised during the 1967 Six Day War when the Arabs established minefields around their cities after attacking Israel so that Dayan's tanks could not penetrate them.

Dayan called his clever design a steel punch: He lined up his battalion of tanks in a row, and one by one they punched through the minefields. The first tank would hit a mine and blow up, and the tank behind it would push it out of the way. Then that next tank would move forward, hit another mine and blow up, and the tank behind that one would push it out of the way. They continued in this manner until they had penetrated the minefields, and the tanks were able to press into the enemy's cities, helping to bring a swift end to the war. The brilliant steel punch paved an iron avenue up which General Dayan's army was able to go to overtake each Arab city in its path.

The Sprague Avenue Ladies

In the Healing Rooms in Spokane, there was a woman named Linda, whom God had healed of HIV. Linda developed within her a burden for Sprague Avenue. Not only did God heal Linda, but He also gave her a vision to begin to step into her destiny and to raise up other ladies who were living out on the streets and had been on drugs and were in desperate need of healing.

As Linda began to do work and to mentor the Sprague Avenue ladies, the Lord began to speak to her. He told her that for Christmas she was to prepare gift baskets for some of the topless dancers who worked at a seedy Sprague Avenue establishment called the Rainbow Club.

Linda came to me and said, "Cal, the Lord has mentioned to me that I am to put together some gift baskets, call up the owner of the Rainbow Club and take these gift baskets to the topless dancers on Christmas Eve."

She asked me what I thought about that, and I said it sounded fine. She then called the bar owner and asked if she could do it. He told her, "Sure. It's the holiday, after all."

So Linda, with the help of some other women, prepared the gift baskets, putting nice little things inside of them that ladies would like and need and appreciate, and wrapping them with cellophane and ribbons.

On Christmas Eve, Linda and the other women went to the Rainbow Club and walked in with the gift baskets. When they entered, the bar owner announced, "Everybody, the Christmas carolers are here."

But Linda responded, "No, we're not Christmas carolers. We have come to give gifts to your dancers."

He was amazed that someone would do something like that. He asked the dancers to stand in a line, and Linda and the women handed a beautiful gift basket to each lady, telling them, "These are gifts from God to you on this holiday."

The bar owner was so taken aback that he hugged Linda and all of the women who came with Linda and thanked each one. "No one's ever come here to give something to these ladies," he told Linda. "They always come and take from them. If there's anything you ever need, Linda, just let me know."

A few weeks later, on Valentine's Day, Linda planned to go back to the Rainbow Club and take roses to the ladies. She told me, "Cal, the Holy Spirit has told me that the Rainbow Club on Sprague Avenue is going to be a church. How can that be?"

"Linda," I responded, "if the Holy Spirit has told you that, you can believe it."

So she began to proclaim that the Rainbow Club was going to become a church. And that Valentine's Day, Linda and her group of women took roses to the Rainbow Club. The bar owner was impressed—and very blessed—that Linda and her women would return again with gifts for the ladies.

Linda said to the bar owner, "Remember the last time we were here and you said that if there was ever anything that I needed I could ask you?" He replied that he did recall his remark. And she said, "Well, there is one thing I need: to have Easter Sunday service here in the bar at the Rainbow Club."

The bar owner answered, "Well . . . I'm going to have to think about that one."

"Okay," said Linda. "I'll call you back."

She didn't want to give him a lot of time to think about it, so she called him the very next day and asked him, "What did you decide? May we hold Easter Sunday service at the club?"

He said, "Well, you've been so nice to me, I don't know how I could refuse you. But you're going to have to get with me and tell me what this is going to look like. Because, after all, this is a topless bar."

So Linda and he discussed the matter, he approved her plan, and she began to make her preparations. She planned to have a worship team onstage where the dancers usually danced. In the middle of the floor area, they would set up tables with white tablecloths. They would have a banquet and serve anyone who entered, including prostitutes, addicts and the homeless. Everyone on Sprague Avenue was going to be invited to join in the Easter Sunday celebration, and testimonies would be shared on how Jesus had transformed lives.

During the time of this preparation, the bar owner took Linda aside and said, "I have a confession to make to you: I used to be a pastor. My wife got sick and died, and I rejected God at that point, but I knew that someday He was going to come back to me." God had begun to move very powerfully upon this man.

Linda continued to make the preparations for the banquet. Local restaurants had heard about what she was doing and told her they wanted to supply all of the food she would need for the Easter Sunday service banquet. They even offered to prepare it all, bring it to the club and set everything up!

On Easter Sunday, everything was ready at the Rainbow Club. The tables were set nicely. The worship team was up on the stage. The dancers had arrived, dressed appropriately for Easter Sunday, and stood behind the bar, serving coffee to everyone. The restaurant brought stainless-steal containers filled with the fancy food. It was so wonderful that we took pictures of the affair.

Then we began the Easter Sunday service. The worship team sang worship songs to Jesus. The intercessors prayed. People shared their testimonies. Addicts and homeless people and prostitutes came in off of the street when they saw the wonderful celebration and banquet taking place. They were welcomed in and couldn't believe that something this good was being done just for them. We even had to take some of them by the hand and lead them to the table, assuring them, "No, this isn't too good for you. This banquet is for you. This is your gift from God." We put a plate in their hands and told them it was a blessing for them to join us and partake of the banquet, because it was God's gift to them on Easter Sunday.

Then a man who had been delivered by God and had come to know Jesus shared his testimony, and people raised their hands to accept the Lord. As the testimony of Jesus began to transform Sprague Avenue during that Easter Sunday service, drug addicts threw down their crack pipes and announced that they were through with drugs.

God's Steel Punch

God had put a steel punch through the darkest place in Spokane: on Sprague Avenue in a topless bar called the Rainbow Club. The light of Jesus came into that dark place as we began to penetrate it and become proactive in taking Jesus into the streets. And He lit it up!

Now Sprague Avenue is the location of Teen Challenge in Spokane. Mending Fences Church moved in. Truth Ministries set up on Sprague Avenue. The Mission now has a women's refuge on the Sprague Avenue strip. The city even began to implement a redevelopment plan for the area.

As the steel punch of God penetrated Sprague Avenue, the door for the light of God to enter into dark places was opened. Sprague Avenue began to heal as the power of the Holy Spirit punched through and overtook it.

It only takes one person to have a vision—one person, like Linda, who is willing to stand in the gap and move the power of the Holy Spirit into a city. That puts the punch in. That punch begins to open the door for the Body of Christ to enter, followed by an activation of the Spirit of God as it is released through the spirit of believers into the darkest places, transforming the entire city.

To see a city transformed is a vision God gives to His people. With God, all things are possible. We have no limits in Him. The Body of Christ must begin to have a vision to see a city healed and then move on that vision.

When we fearlessly, lovingly penetrate a city, we open it up for healing.

THE MOVE FROM UNISON TO UNITY

After 2,000 years, the Church is more divided than we are united. We have a desire that comes from the Holy Spirit to unify the Body of Christ, but an entrenched denominationalism has separated us. The fact that Christians meet within a denomination is an expression that we have a theology that's different from another group of Christians—and that represents *division*. Churches across the street from each other don't even fellowship together. The Bible says that a house divided cannot stand (see Matthew 12:25; Luke 11:17). We need a unity that is set in spirit and in faith.

Healing Rooms does conferences all over the world, and we have been mightily blessed seeing movements of different denominations begin to come together in unity. Thankfully, many are now striving to join, in one way or another, as brothers and sisters in Christ. In cities all over the world, there is a movement by the Holy Spirit to draw the Body of Christ together no matter the different denominations.

Ephesians 4:13 tells us that we are to reach unity in the faith and in the knowledge of Christ, and to become mature, attaining to the whole measure "the fullness of Christ." But for too long the Church has resisted this. Rather than meeting as a five-fold Body of Christ, the Church has been meeting as a threefold Body, where only pastors, teachers and evangelists come together in cities. And when different denominations *have* gotten together, the Holy Spirit hasn't always been invited to the meetings—maybe the Pentecostal pastor didn't want to offend the evangelical pastor. That may have established *unison* of people, but it did not bring *unity* in spirit.

We must invite the power of the Holy Spirit into the mix in order to create a sustaining unity that gives the Body of Christ a vision to see cities joined and transformed. If we don't embrace the power of the Holy Spirit to bring signs, wonders and miracles to a lost generation, then we're not going to have a sign that leads them to Jesus.

The unity effort (particularly in America) has begun to unravel because people don't want to offend each other, and they tiptoe around theological topics that they need to join together in discussing and seeking out common ground. When they don't do this, churches establish a mere acquaintance with each other; this doesn't have enough power or depth to sustain a relationship, and it gradually falls apart. The churches drift into merely conducting meetings and having retreats and luncheons—coming together as leaders, but not truly joining forces in real vision, and with no united effort to see their city fully transformed. In a couple of decades of this type of "effort," we haven't seen one single city truly and fully transformed in America.

It was never God's plan for Earth and heaven to be separated, for separation between the seen and the unseen. God cannot have fellowship with believers if there is a chasm between us, if we are cut off from one another. There must be a renewed effort—one that embraces the Holy Spirit so that the Body of Christ can move in unity and power. When we become united in spirit, we will begin to discover that the lost *and* the cities are worth our very lives. Then the Church will become a united, harvesting Church that thinks "us," rather than a Church set in a rapture mentality that thinks "me."

If a house divided cannot stand, then surely a house united will not fall.

The Move from Rapture Mentality to Harvest Theology

Adam walked and talked intimately with God until the Fall. Jesus, the second Adam, came to restore that intimacy and link us back to God. That link comes through the filling of the Holy Spirit within the Body of Christ, the result of which is that God's will is fulfilled in the natural realm, causing the supernatural and the natural realm to become one again.

Separating the two realms causes us to have what I call a "rapture mentality" rather than a *harvest theology*. The rapture mentality says that we can't have a demonstration of God's power here and now and that the only kingdom we will ever experience is a future Kingdom when Jesus returns for His Bride. But Matthew 6:9-10 disproves this mindset, as Jesus told us: "Pray then in this way: 'Our Father in heaven, hallowed be your name. Your kingdom come. Your will be done, on earth as it is in heaven'" (*NSRV*). As believers, we are to bring the kingdom of God to Earth by demonstrating His will and His power through our everyday lives. To do this, we must move from a rapture mentality to a harvest theology.

Ultimately, when we get to heaven, we're not going to need God's Word, because we will be in the presence of *the* Word—Jesus Christ Himself (see John 1:1). But here and now, we *do* need to fulfill the will of God as shown in His Word.

As we submit to the Holy Spirit, His power brings a demonstration into our lives that backs up the truth of God's Word (see Hebrews 2:3-5). This kinetic power in our lives is God's evidence, His *revelation*, that the Word is true and lives in us (see 1 Corinthians 2:4-5). This revelation produces transformation in our lives, and this transformation then triggers activation of God's Word. The end result of this activation is a demonstration to others of God's power through us.

A Demonstrated Power

The Body of Christ must become a Body that goes to church on Sunday looking to establish healing in the Body so that the Body can then establish healing in cities. We must become a harvesting Church that has a strategy to come together for the benefit of taking the harvest in cities—not with everybody operating to fulfill their own separate agenda, but joining together in power, unity and authority.

The Body of Christ must begin to move into a Kingdom understanding that we have authority over all the power of our enemy: No weapon formed by the devil against us is going to prosper. We are not going to be overcome by what the enemy does to mess our cities up. We *are* going to overcome the enemy so that we can see cities transformed and the harvest reaped.

We must have a demonstration of the power of God in the Body of Christ so that the Body of Christ can demonstrate His power to the lost (see 1 Corinthians 2:4-5). The lost need a sign that leads them to Jesus. This is why the Bible says that these signs shall follow us, that we shall lay hands on the sick and they shall recover (see Mark 16:17-18). This is why Paul said, "My message and my preaching were not in persuasive words of wisdom, but in demonstration of the Spirit and of power, that your faith should not rest on the wisdom of men, but on the power of God" (1 Corinthians 2:4-5).

The Church doesn't need a sign—the lost need a sign. The Church already knows how to get to the city of God. Only a person unfamiliar with the way needs a sign. The Church must begin to give the lost the sign and to lead the way.

In the New Testament, Jesus was always bringing a sign—a sign for a healing, a sign for a miracle that would show the lost who He was. We need a sign today—a demonstration of God's power in the Body of Christ so that we can show cities how to get to Jesus.

God established the world for His people to have dominion over. Yet we do not have a united strategy for a vision to see cities transformed. We have not moved in unity. Because of that, we lack power. We talk too much about the rapture—how soon we can get out—rather than how many we can bring in.

A Harvesting Church

A harvesting church fulfills the will of God in this realm because it brings His kingdom into the city; and His will is fulfilled when we heal the sick, cleanse the diseased, raise the dead and lead the lost to the Lord. This will move us from worrying about whether or not we will be raptured out to emphasizing our pulling the end-time harvest *in*. Jesus is not coming for a Church in failure. He's coming for a Church in victory, a Church that has taken the final harvest.

> Then I looked, and behold, a white cloud, and sitting on the cloud was one like a son of man, having a golden crown on His head, and a sharp sickle in His hand. And another angel came out of the temple, crying out with a loud voice to Him who sat on the cloud, "Put in your sickle and reap, for the hour to reap has come, because the harvest of the earth is ripe." And He who sat on the cloud swung His sickle over the earth, and the earth was reaped (Revelation 14:14-16).

GOD'S STRATEGY FOR A

Healing

TRANSFORMATION

When God spoke to us about Spokane and showed us how He could put the steel punch into Sprague Avenue and light up the city, He said, "I want to give you the strategy to see your city transformed."

At this writing, Spokane's Healing Rooms Ministries have over 600 Healing Rooms in close to 40 nations. God clearly instructed us, "Not only do I want to see healing in the Body of Christ all over the world, but also I want to see My Body begin to bring healing to cities all over the world. I'm going to give you a strategy. And you won't see the whole strategy in the beginning, but as you begin to step into it, I'll begin to reveal it to you."

So He called us to begin what we call ACTS Ministries. ACTS is an acronym for Apostolic Center for Training and Service.

God said, "I want you to take those ministries in the city that deal with prostitution, homelessness, addiction, wayward youth—all of these issues—and begin to equip the Body of Christ and empower those ministries in what they do because the people that have been called to work with the homeless on the street, the people who are called to work with prostitutes, those who are working with the youth—all of these different ministries are out on the street and so often they are struggling to survive because they don't get the support from the Body of Christ that they need."

ACTS Ministries is an equipping center geared totally to city transformation—we bring many different ministries together, creating a network. Currently we have 25 different ministries around the city that we network together and support. Each Saturday night at our ACTS meetings, we have worship, we have a message, and we have training. To keep us linked and informed, we have a newsletter that goes out to all the network's different worldwide ministries, detailing the various strategies used to see cities impacted.

The Holy Spirit told us that we Christians don't have a right to *transform* a city until we learn how to *serve* a city. He said, "I want you to create a foundation called Serve the City Foundation. This is not going to be about being in the *face* of the lost but being in the *heart* of the lost." It was to be about learning how to serve them so that they could realize what the heart of Jesus is like, so that they would be drawn in. So we established the Serve the City Foundation, a nonprofit organization.

Then the Holy Spirit said, "I want you to develop a coalition of marketplace businesspeople who are Christians filled with the Holy Spirit." The coalition meets monthly at a luncheon and oversees the distribution of the funds for the Serve the City Foundation. The funds that are raised are sent out to the networked ministries. The ACTS people find out the needs of the 25 networked ministries—one might need tires for a ministry van, another might need money for a particular outreach effort. Each request is brought to the coalition, which then makes the final decision regarding how best to meet the need.

First, we track down materials before we spend money. For example, if someone needs tires for a van, we have some of our ACTS people go to a local tire store and visit with the manager. They tell the manager the vision of ACTS and what the service is all about. Then they ask the manager if they can pray that this would be the most successful tire store in the city. What's a good businessperson going to say to that—"No"? They always respond, "Yes!" Many even donate the tires. Those tires are then taken by our ACTS people to the ministry and given to them.

When materials are pursued first, the funds in the Serve the City Foundation can go farther to meet the needs of the networked ministries during the year. This has begun to impact the city of Spokane as we empower those ministries that do the work God has called them to. This effort has had such an impact in Spokane that the mayor has come to us and requested information on our ministry.

We first met the mayor at our Serve the City Foundation annual fundraiser, where 300 businesspeople came together, and we cast the vision and raised the money for the foundation. These businesspeople—even though they may not all be Christians—realized that there is a benefit with having prostitution ended, homelessness abated and wayward youth brought back to their homes. These actions benefit the local businesses, who want to sow into those efforts, whether they're Christian or not.

At the Serve the City Foundation fundraisers, we share testimonies on how lives are transformed by these ministries. This has had a tremendous impact on local businesspeople.

When the mayor visited with me, I explained to him what we were doing in the city; and he said, "I want to be involved. I want to know about it. I want to play a part in it."

He told us that the city government sets up programs that might change the minds of people for a while, but that we had something different, something that is changing people's hearts permanently, moving them from where they were to where they lead productive lives. He told us that the city needs to play a part in something that transforms lives and creates a lasting and significant legacy. The mayor's support opened a door for us to begin to show the city through servanthood that we have something in Jesus that brings a benefit and healing to the city that the government cannot accomplish.

It's simple, really: It's Jesus, changing people's lives one heart at a time.

HEALING FOR *ALL* PEOPLE

One day a staff intercessor came to me and said, "Cal, they're having a psychic fair down at the City Center." She explained that 4,000 psychics come together there every year. She asked if a booth for our ACTS people could be set up with a sign that read "Prophetic Readings and Prayer for Healing." A tent would cover the booth, and the intercessors would be available to pray and prophesy over people who came inside.

I said, "Sure! Let's go for it!" because the light of Jesus belongs in darkness, in the streets, not just in the church.

The intercessors prayed that at the psychic fair they would have an impact and that the anointing of Christ would flow. They set up the tent, they prayed, and intercessors called down Holy Spirit fire—and psychics and witches and Wiccans began to come in because they felt something there: They felt a *power*! All of these New Age people gathered at the only tent with a long line in front of it at the entire Convention Center: ours!

As soon as these New Age people came into the presence of the Holy Spirit inside our tent, they began to weep, saying, "What is this? We sense power and love here. We want to have the power that you have."

As our intercessors shared Jesus, people lined up for healing and accepted the Lord as their Savior! The testimony of Jesus began to prophesy. People watched God demonstrate His power, and the light came into the dark place as psychics came to Jesus and became born again.

The power of God belongs in the city. The lost have a right to receive what God has. We must not hang on to what God has given us; we must learn to release it into our cities so that there will be a transformation.

It's only because we lack vision that we don't move into the city, and people without a vision will perish (see Proverbs 29:18). When we have a vision for a city, we begin to move into our destiny—a destiny of seeing lives transformed.

It has taken us 2,000 years to figure out that we come into a place of being born again and we go to church so that we can get prepared to *go out into all the world and minister the gospel*. Why has it taken so many Christians so long to figure that out? We seem to have been waiting around for the lost to come to us—

but the lost have been waiting for us to come to them! They're more ready to receive Jesus than we've been prepared to get Him to them. We must GO!

> Go therefore and make disciples of *all the nations,* baptizing them in the name of the Father and the Son and the Holy Spirit, teaching them to observe all that I commanded you; and lo, I am with you always, even to the end of the age (Matthew 28:19-20, emphasis added).

The greatest adventure that a Christian can ever have is to see the power of God demonstrated to the lost in a city, then see the city transformed and then see that transformation bring people into our churches so that they can be equipped and then sent out into their own city.

HEALING FOR ALL HIS LAND

The Lord first began to stir me about healing the land when we opened Healing Rooms Ministries on July 22, 1999. I was driving downtown, over the Maple Street Bridge. Driving over the Spokane River across the bridge provides a view of the city. On that particular day, I was driving very early in the morning, and it was still fairly dark outside. And I had an open vision . . .

I had never really had an open vision like that before, but it was one of those cases where you are 10 miles down the road, and you don't really know how you got there. As this open vision began to unfold, I found myself hovering over the city of Spokane, slowly being raised upward. I saw flashes of light above my head; the city was dark, but the sky was being pierced with flashes of light. I wondered what they were.

As I was raised up, I came up over the mountaintops around the city of Spokane, and I saw white horses—as far as the eye could see. On every horse, there was a warrior, and every warrior held a sword. Lightning was flashing from the tip of the sword each warrior held.

As I viewed this vast army, they began to ride. Soon, the advancing army began to crest the hill to descend into the city, the horses' hooves pounding the earth with such force that the ground began to shake. As the ground shook, the enemy began to tremble. Then the horses descended into the city, the lightning flashes from the warriors' swords striking across the sky to such a degree that it glowed as the thundering hooves advanced.

As the sky lit up, the windows of heaven began to roll back. As they rolled back, from heaven I heard a voice like a roaring lion, a voice like thunder: "Let My people go!"

I believe this vision God had given me was a prophetic picture of the end-time Church taking Spokane for Jesus and healing cities around the world.

THE ARMY OF GOD

It's the army of God, carrying the sword of the Spirit, that will allow the lightning and fire of God to come into every city and light it up as lives are transformed by the Word of truth as God wields the sword with power and authority in the hand of every believer.

We must become a harvesting Church!

We must become a harvesting army!

We must begin to have a vision for our city that is as big as heaven!

We must begin to realize that the power of the Holy Spirit in us is not only enough to transform our own lives, but it also is enough to transform entire cities!

We must no longer limit God. We have a truth that sets us free. In order to accomplish this, we must get everything out of the way that has blocked healing from the Body of Christ. If the Body of Christ cannot be healed, then how can the Body heal a city? If we have defilement in us, then there will be defilement in the city. But we can bring healing to the city, because we have been given the power of God over this realm. We have been "redeemed . . . from the curse of the Law" (Galatians 3:13).

Faith is the creative power of God in us to bring fulfillment of the Word upon the earth.

We are a supernatural people because *we are created in the image of God.* We can rise up and wear the armor of God that will extinguish all the fiery darts of the enemy. We are a people who are not moved by a spirit of religion, but by a spirit of revelation. We can bring the government of God into this realm.

Love, which comes from God (and *is* God, according to 1 John 4:8 and 4:16), is mighty and irresistible and powerful.

We are redeemed as a harvesting army that must become a warring force against what the enemy does to devastate God's people. We must set the captives free. The lost are worth everything we have.

I don't know about you, but when I read the last chapter of God's Book, I learned that we win! But something has to happen between now and then: We have to rise into our destiny. And our destiny is not polishing a pew with the seat of our pants. Our destiny is out on the streets, out among the people, out there with God's creation. Jesus said that the second greatest commandment of all is that we must *love our neighbor as ourselves* (see Matthew 22:39).

The church must become an equipping place. We must come to church to equip and then to release what God has given us as He moves us into the city—whether it's in our workplace, in our business, at the marketplace—no matter where it is.

We cannot have a wedding until the Bride of Christ moves out of failure and into victory. The King is coming for a Bride that is without spot or wrinkle—a Bride that is not a failure but a victory, a Bride who is fulfilling the will of God on Earth and moving in the authority that God has given us to transform cities. As the Bride of Christ, we cannot afford to be so busy fighting our own problems that we don't have time for the lost.

Let's not read one thing in the Bible and live another in our lives. Let's live out what we read. Will you commit to start *now*, *today*, to live in the realm of the Word of truth and move it from ink on paper to *action* in your life?

We, as the Bride of Jesus, must come to a place where we no longer choose to accept being sick. Ours is a God with no sickness in Him—and *we* are in Him! Therefore, there should be no sickness in us. He wants us to receive all of our inheritance so that His kingdom can come upon Earth as it is in heaven. The only limit heaven has is *us*. The only things between heaven and

Earth are you and me. God wants us involved in bringing all of Him to all of the earth, in all of His power, His miracles and His healing.

> "For you who fear My name, the sun of righteousness will rise with healing in its wings; and you will go forth and skip about like calves from the stall. You will tread down the wicked, for they shall be ashes under the soles of your feet on the day which I am preparing," says the LORD of hosts (Malachi 4:2-3).

ACKNOWLEDGMENTS

This work and my destiny are intricately entwined with my wife, Michelle. She is my constant companion, both at home and at conferences. Michelle intercedes for me and for the work of healing around the world. Her unfailing love and commitment sets the stage for Holy Spirit revelation, signs and wonders. I am forever grateful to the Lord for the treasure I have in her.

I would also like to thank the following people for their involvement in this work:

Pam Yates—Thanks for transcribing my materials into word form. It was a labor of love. Thank you.

Marie McMichael, my administrator—Thanks for your encouragement that got me through the process, and your tireless effort in reviewing the work. You are a blessing to me.

To our staff—Thank you for your excellence and dedication in stewarding this work around the world. It is your love for Jesus that inspires me.

To the Healing Rooms teams in Spokane and around the world—Thank you, for you are doing the work. You are an example of what ordinary people can do to become extraordinary. You are changing the world as history makers.

I love you all!

—Dad

ABOUT THE AUTHOR

Cal Pierce, a member of the International Coalition of Apostles, was told by the Holy Spirit, "There is a time to pray and a time to move." And moving is exactly what Cal has been doing since July 1999, when he opened Healing Rooms Ministries in Spokane, Washington.

The Healing Rooms are places to come and receive prayer for any need. Healing Rooms offer a safe place where God's love and healing power are present.

But the vision given to Cal was much larger than for just one location, so he birthed the International Association of Healing Rooms, which now has over 700 Healing Rooms operating in close to 40 nations. As the International Director, Cal is active in spreading the message of healing through conferences and training seminars throughout the world.

Cal and his wife, Michelle, travel extensively, always ready to share the great news of healing in the kingdom of God with all whom they encounter.

More Great Resources From
Regal Books

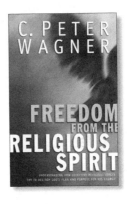